#INTEGRITY

Developing a Principled Life

Koby Bryan

#INTEGRITY
Developing a Principled Life
Copyright © 2014 Koby Bryan. All rights reserved.

Cover Design: Shake Creative www.shaketampa.com

ISBN: 0-9907448-0-9
ISBN-13: 978-0-9907448-0-1

DEDICATION

There are many along the way that deserve credit. My friends and colleagues for pushing me to write... my editor Jan Powell for making the process fun!

I dedicate this to my parents, Jim and Laverne Bryan for bringing me in the world and lovingly shaping who I am.

To my brother Mark Bryan for always being there, supportive without question.

To my wife Martina Bryan for loving the man I have become, and for the excitement of being able to share the rest of our journey together as partners.

To all of those who strive to demonstrate a life of virtue and absolutely refuse to be broken.

#INTEGRITY Developing a Principled Life

WHY IS A "#" IN THE TITLE?

Social media is a term that can define many software networks like Google+, Facebook and Twitter; among others that are popular at the time of this printing. Especially within these networks, a *hashtag*—the phrase or mini-sentence immediately preceded by the pound sign (#)—has a special meaning.

A key way to categorize your information online is to attach a *tag* to your communication, which is a kind of label. This allows you to turn whatever you post on these networks into discussion topics, as the entire tag becomes a *link*, called a *hashtag*. You can then click on this link to see all posts with that tag or subject in real time, as others post and tag their own information.

Join the community online that shares and collaborates on developing a life of principles, and stay up-to-date with new information and resources on integrity.

If this book inspires you and you would like to share, it's easy. You can tag a quote by your favorite author, personal phrase or any post online that you feel in any way relates to integrity and this book, by typing "#IntegrityBook" *and* "#Integrity" in your post—as in this example:

Do the right thing, especially when nobody is watching. #IntegrityBook #Integrity

FOR MORE PLEASE VISIT

www.integritybook.com

CONTENTS

#INTEGRITY Developing a Principled Life

PART I:
BEGINNING

My eighteenth birthday. February 22, 1991. The events that occurred were none I'd ever have anticipated or planned. The unexpected blow hit me so hard that I found myself seeing stars, not imaginary ones, but the actual sky. Survival instincts immediately kicked in. Pure logic replaced pain, with only reaction left.

Stunned, I didn't know if I was standing on my feet or lying on my back. If I was on the ground, I was determined to get up, but if I was standing I intended to remain erect. In boxing, they call this punch a *bell ringer*, but this was no sporting strike. This *sucker punch*, a surprise blow, crushed the bones in my face and thrust my nose underneath my left eye.

My personal reasons for writing come from my passion for integrity. Peers pushed me to do this because the way I live is unusual and noteworthy. After deep consideration, I elected to put myself under a microscope of analysis and tell significant stories from my life. Before now, I only told close friends these incidents, to avoid sounding like a braggart. My upbringing cautioned against spilling my life out in front of others. Humility is not meant to be another form of pride.

Recently a close friend convinced me to record these things. "Koby, regardless of what you think, you could be robbing someone of a deeper understanding or healing who has gone through similar experiences."

These events provide context for my behavior and beliefs. My insights here are yours for the taking. Draw your own conclusions and gain some value. You decide.

I grew up in a rough, rural Florida town. Most families had World War II veterans, survivors of heavy combat, with trigger reactions to the perception of threatening situations. They were quick to take offense and strike out to insure a loved one's safety or preserve respect. Mine was no exception, with grandfathers on both sides of my family as veterans.

Dad worked hard as a lineman and Mom did healthcare management. That meant we juggled holidays and celebrations around their schedules. We planned to celebrate my birthday a few days later although this was the actual day I turned eighteen.

I was home alone that day when my friend, Joe, came over. I often slept through the afternoon and stayed up late. With little entertainment available and no money to spend, we'd wander through the orange groves at night because nature was free.

He arrived while my parents were still out and woke me from sleep. I came to, startled and panicked.

He noticed. "What the hell happened? Are you okay?"

"I…don't know. I had a nightmare." I rubbed my eyes and scanned the room to reassure myself of my bearings. "I can't remember what it was about though. It's freaking me out."

He gave my shoulder a playful shove. "Aw, come on. You're fine. Are you ready to go?"

"I feel really terrible, like something bad is going to happen." I shook my head and looked him straight in the eyes. "It's like Death himself is near. I can't shake the feeling."

I wasn't religious, but felt seriously afraid. I thought my dream was a premonition. After more talk I suggested a plan. "Listen. Give me exactly thirty minutes. We'll use the oven timer. If I can't think of one logical reason why we shouldn't go out, I'll get my sh*t together and we'll go. Okay?" Thirty minutes came and went. The timer buzzed. By now, I felt more alert and in control, so we left.

It was a clear evening with a big star-spattered sky. Walking two blocks from home, we discussed the movie *Dances with Wolves* with Kevin Costner. A military man sent to a remote western Civil War outpost, goes wild and lives among the Indians. We loved Native American culture, because Joe had Native American ancestry. He was descended from a great American naturalist of the late 1700's who took a Native American as the mother of his children. This radical choice of that time didn't make the history books, although we were required to read about his ancestor in high school.

A jeep coming down the road angled toward us. I said. "Close one eye so we won't be totally blind when the headlights get closer or if anything happens." The rowdy people in the jeep sped past hollering at us.

Joe yelled back a friendly, "Hey!" as though he knew them.

They slammed on their brakes a short distance away. From their shouted profanities, it appeared doubtful that Joe knew them, or that they were friendly.

We stopped. Joe looked between me and the nearby jeep. "What should we do?"

Experience in the country meant they could have guns, knives, anything. We had no way of knowing. With my skin prickling warning and my stomach clenching I glanced around. "We should run!" With that, I took off, clearly the smartest choice.

Joe stood his ground. He was a nice guy, late to mature, and shorter than me in the past but now, taller and strong. In his family, compared with his brothers and younger sister, he ranked on the bottom of the blame hierarchy. His parents expended so much time trying to keep them out of trouble that since he wasn't a troublemaker, they *gave* him trouble. He reminded me of a crab in a bucket. When one almost escapes to freedom, the rest pull that one back down, so they share a mutual death. He was that crab.

His violent home, filled with rough young men, issued him a learner's permit to hell—figuring out how to avoid attachment to anything that people could use against him. I wondered how he survived, striving to become different, trying to better himself, and all the while he was like an alien among them.

Back then, no one could predict his younger sister's choices; I hoped she'd be okay. His devious twin brother paid early for his pure evil with a jail sentence; perhaps that restriction saved his life. As we say in the south, "Bless his heart."

In our town, the police generally arrived after forty-five minutes, if you were lucky. This left you on your own in matters of personal safety. Most violence erupted and ended in three minutes. We knew this.

Joe decided not to run. Sick and tired of all the crap he was getting at home, he determined this would be the moment to make a stand. Seventy yards down the road, I realized I was running alone. He remained rooted by the road yelling back and forth with the guys in the jeep, trying to reason with them. Clearly they intended to hurt someone badly.

I took a moment to weigh the consequences of returning. If he was going to get killed, I wouldn't let him go out alone. This choice went against everything my dad had taught me since I was big enough to make a fist. I raced back, once again closing one eye as I ran toward the headlights. They saw me coming and pulled the jeep beside me in order to look me over.

They yelled, "Hey! Are you a dude or a chick?"

I laughed, too cocky at that moment for a guy with long hair. "I'm a 'dude'."

They jerked to a halt, noisily put on the emergency brake, and rushed toward me. What happened wasn't a true fight for I threw no punches. Nor was it a mugging because they took no money. As the fast-moving, small one approached, I readied myself. I glimpsed a flash in his hand. Knife? Gun? His left hand gripped a beer bottle, a potentially deadly weapon, and his right clenched into a fist.

When one guy started throwing savage punches at Joe, he fled into the path of the headlights with his attacker in hot pursuit. I couldn't count them. Were there two, three or four? I tried to block the little guy's punches and keep an eye on his bottle, but it was too dark. He was backlit by the jeeps headlights and I was getting pounded in my ribs and stomach.

The sudden, crunching strike had me dizzy, looking at the stars. That critical blow came from another guy who ran hard at me in the dark, while I focused on the beer-bottle wielding guy. I'd become a sitting duck, vulnerable to hits by two or more people. I tried to back away and put distance between us to gauge the situation and the numbers we faced. I was fighting for my life, vulnerable, uncertain of my fate.

Their quick action and greater numbers, fueled by drink and aggression, overwhelmed us. We were easy targets, attacked without reason, ignorant of their intentions. I remained upright, but uneasy. I could not go down! I had to remain standing at all costs.

While swiftly evaluating the situation and backing away, my feet caught the curb, sending me down in a heap. Flashes of death raced through my mind… kicking, stomping, or a bottle to the head. Maybe stabbing, a baseball bat, or the crack of a gun. During a lull in the violence, one of the attackers climbed into the jeep and sat on the passenger side and opened the glove compartment. I thought he was getting a gun.

I had an opportunity to act and made a decision that changed my life.

I decided to kill, then and there.

I knew this was a very serious choice, one I never thought I'd make. I'd never be able to take it back, no matter the consequences, but I believed that living beyond this dark encounter was more important. If I was going to save my life and rescue my friend, desperate action must follow. You can't settle for merely wounding or trying to incapacitate an attacker when your life is threatened, wounded people can still kill you.

As a teenager I carried a five-inch knife on me. I reached for it before I thought they could finish me off. I knew my initial target—the person who hit me first. I'd only taken my eyes off of him for a moment, but knew him with absolute certainty by his silhouette and height. He was the one now sitting in the jeep, looking for something. I had to be fast.

But my back pocket was empty. I'd given Joe the knife before we left the house because my nightmare convinced me that if anything happened, I was likely to use it.

With no weapon and uncertain of Joe's location, I decided to run. I'd eliminate their advantage of numbers and headlights using the cover of dark. I gagged on the blood I was inhaling as I sped away. It poured like a hose inside my head. I hoped it might be tears running down my face, but the light of a street lamp revealed more blood on my clothes than I had ever seen. I was drenched.

When Joe caught up with me he only had a minor black eye. After one look at me he said, "Your face, it's really bad. Emergency room bad."

Once home I ran water over my clothes in the tub and drove myself to the hospital. Joe lobbied for an ambulance, but I thought I was controlling the bleeding. I'd optimistically attempted to "fix" my nose. Big mistake! The mushy bones sounded and felt hideous, like I was manipulating a crunchy clay face, that couldn't be my own.

Why did I give my knife away before leaving that evening? When risk may arise and a ready means of protection seems sensible, an odd response is to disarm, right?

My father taught me to fight since I was big enough to make a fist. He valued personal protection, loved his family passionately, and equipped me to survive the best way he could. The skills he instilled weren't for sport or exercise, but for combat and defense, playing for keeps.

Dad taught street fighting. He ran classes for soldiers, cops, and people interested in surviving deadly violence. His classes gave no awards or colored belts for winning. There were few rules and no real referee—your reward was you lived another day, the best prize after a desperate confrontation.

His friends and mentors were Special Operations soldiers, former mercenaries, CIA, undercover police officers, people in gang enforcement; the list goes on and on. These extremists put their lives on the line to protect our freedom and way of life. Being raised in a rural setting, I knew how to shoot. Before I reached fourteen, I added other skills like: Thai Kickboxing (Muay Thai), knife fighting, and stick fighting.

On my fourteenth birthday a friend of my dad's, a suspected covert CIA agent, gave me an icepick as a gift and taught me how to most effectively kill someone during a self-protection seminar at his house. (He was later killed in the USA and the government squashed all news about it.)

Because actions have life-changing consequences, motives behind these choices need careful and disciplined consideration. Bad people usually have bad lives with violent endings. By contrast, good people generally have good lives, regardless of how they end. Good people who are extreme or specialist warriors tend to have shorter lives.

By giving Joe my knife, I changed the course of my life. I deliberately chose to disarm myself, knowing my nerves were on edge. I hoped my trained instincts would prove effective in a life or death situation. A weapon would be too easy to rely on when careful thought might be necessary. It felt like a gamble, but I wasn't ready to use a weapon against someone—if you can ever be ready for that possibility.

Florida laws support a response with deadly force if you believe that your life is threatened. In 1991, I don't know if a deadly response would have been *justified*. Taking a life isn't like a TV a drama or the movies. You carry the consequences with you forever. Intimate details about your attacker remain in your mind, even if it was a stranger who targeted you as a victim. This burden of accountability as a lawful member of society comes from having and using a conscience. Any fight, including one where you're morally right, where others view you as the good guy, doesn't mean you'll win, unlike the movies. I've seen plenty of confident people, fueled by righteousness, emerge badly injured losers in a confrontation.

Years after my assault, I don't over analyze the motivations that lead someone to victimize another. Ultimately, there's only one reason: they think they can get away with it. My experience indicates it's rarely personal. They just succumb to base drives, let emotions take over, and discard any rational thinking. They justify their actions and ignore the moral mess created. It applies to the red-light runner who nearly hits you, and then glares and gestures like you were the one at fault. That happens daily and it's not personal.

During the fight, I was so intent on the attack that only later did I remember two girls in the jeep screaming for them to stop. At the time of the fight, they were invisible to my perception. My focus on surviving blocked them, but they were important witnesses to the events.

I escaped when I ran, but went back and reentered the situation for Joe. Though it seems unfair, when I returned out of concern for him, I could have been considered the aggressor since I left and went back. This legal interpretation would have been disastrous if I'd killed someone. It could have been determined in court that I should have abandoned him to his fate, even death.

Life is never simple. Under intense scrutiny, the girls may have testified contrary to the truth to protect themselves from underage drinking, or to shield a boyfriend's memory.

Luckily for us, the girls were spotted earlier at the

only convenience store in the area by a friend of my brother. Under police pressure, they disclosed all the details and the two attackers were caught and charged.

I don't think they spent any time in jail and don't remember because I never went to court. My mother went in my place with photos of my damaged face for evidence. My father decided to trust the law to do what was right, but he thoroughly investigated my attackers. I believe Dad and his friends concluded they were stupid kids out looking for a thrill, and not genuinely bad people.

In my home town, bad things eventually happened to bad people. People occasionally took the law into their own hands, although this happened more during my dad's youth than mine. The law also was very strictly enforced.

Our Sheriff Grady Judd got national attention when a reporter asked him why his deputies shot a murderer sixty-eight times. This man had killed a deputy during a routine traffic stop, shooting the officer eight times, including behind the ear at close range, execution style, then wounded another deputy and killed a police dog during a later manhunt. Sheriff Judd answered, "Because that's all the ammunition we had."

When I was in college, I received a large amount of money later, as a result of the attack. When I had reconstructive surgery, I acquired a more fashionable nose that made me better looking. I still had to reconcile the fact that I'd decided to kill a man and acted, even though I didn't hurt anyone. Without personal rules and careful consideration about how I'd conduct myself in life, I was absolutely terrified. Another crazy situation or random chance encounter could go from bad to worse based on a single decision I might make. I worried about choices that might waste my life and turn my dreams, hopes, and desires to dust. I had carefully considered the consequences of my actions before, but the night I turned eighteen cemented the importance of thinking before acting.

The evening of February 22, 1991 was my passage into manhood, my commitment to do the right thing even at my own expense, and to always strive to live a life of integrity.

PART II:
INTEGRITY IS NEEDED NOW

Things are moving faster, memories grow shorter, and everything is immediate and customized. The information age has evolved into an era where people expect free information. In previous decades people paid hundreds of dollars for a tape series. Now that same material, updated and improved, with a better video format, can be acquired without cost on the internet.

Advertisers seek more creative ways to deliver their messages. Companies invest billions to learn details about consumers in order to enhance the persuasive power of their messages. In fact, businesses now conceal their accumulated knowledge, to avoid what the industry calls the *creep factor*.

One well-known example is a father's complaint regarding maternity care information mailed to his teenage daughter. He didn't know that researchers had identified her behavior and purchases as indicating she might be pregnant. Later he called back to apologize because she really *was* pregnant. However, the corporation and advertising industry at large had discovered that *being creepy* that way made consumers *less* likely to buy and triggered other negative reactions. As a result, they randomly mix maternity care items with other sale items to suggest their advertisements weren't tailored to particular buyers. Targeted advertisements are so incredibly made-to-order, that now it's possible they can be *too customized.*

Politicians and world leaders follow the modern pace and cultivate short memories among their voters. Historians know world leaders took great care to assist America's allies and enemies following World War II. They helped rebuild the infrastructure and aided reconstruction. More importantly, they insured cultural dignity and worked to prevent humiliating poverty. Although the enemies and their ideology were punished, they clearly separated that punishment from the civilians and the culture of the defeated nations.

Why is this noteworthy? World War II was a war of extermination. The Nazis and Imperial Japanese often destroyed the property and killed the citizens of the defeated territories. They eradicated whole towns and classes of people they believed were beneath them. Americans and our allies didn't discriminate civilians from combatants in the atomic bombings of Japanese cities either. Hiroshima and Nagasaki were reduced to a hellish landscape, leaving disfigured and melted civilian survivors coughing up blood, waiting to die. Now, when more precise control of bombs might kill only a few civilians, the opinion of many in our country turns against it in activism.

Why did world leaders try to help the defeated nations? They learned from World War I that defeated, humiliated people become susceptible to bitterness and hatred. This fertile environment seduces people into willing support for vicious and prideful dictators like Hitler. The result was a war so horrific that everyone wanted to avoid all possibilities of repeating those mistakes for future generations. A long term memory of these events was required, unlike today.

Our modern despised enemy is the terrorist. Today world leaders choose to exterminate the leaders of an unpopular nation without considering the long term consequences. They know memory will fade with the passing news cycle. Few become alarmed that this action will leave the defeated in humiliating poverty.

Swift battles don't win wars against numerous faceless terrorists when attempting to break the power of an entire group of people. Quite the contrary, killing a few terrorists creates martyrs and breeds even more in a battle of ideology. Sadly, the world's militaries are rediscovering the lessons earlier politicians learned that were then forgotten. It has been said, "Those who don't learn from the past are doomed to repeat it." Sometimes the stable enemy you know is better than the unstable, desperate one you don't.

The way common goods are bought and sold now supports this new collective, short-term memory. Products are customized rather than being mass produced. Personal service and customization supersede sales of general items off the shelf. Creative innovations are celebrated over the old factory idea of mass production of identical goods.

People rent or lease instead of buying, including the actual personnel in the corporate world. The demand for temporary workers through staffing companies continues to rise at an alarming rate. Healthcare reform in the United States makes a salaried worker less attractive than a contract or temporary one. As the number of entrepreneurs increases, they become the spearhead of a popular movement for change, and some call this a revolution. Consumers want the best of everything when, where and how they like it.

The smartphone has become a common international personal accessory. Each user customizes the display with his personal preferences.

It expresses the owner's personality in a similar way as image is expressed on social networks. In addition, 3D printers enable people to create manufactured items at home. E-book readers and the tools of the internet permit tweaking to suit the tastes and whims of readers.

Our culture and media promote a cut-throat, short-sighted, and self-centered emphasis on winning as a virtue. We desire it over everything, even at the expense of integrity. With deception and a bottom-line strategy, cheating has become accepted when people get paid for performance alone. Getting caught has become a considered risk in playing the game. Increasing high-profile corporate scandals no longer shock, particularly because the wrong-doers skirt punishment. They rarely receive severe penalties the public believes they deserve because they are *too big to fail.* CEO's get replaced, billions are levied in fines and lost business—until the company goes through a re-branding and the cycle starts once more. Risk-taking with catastrophic train-wrecks at the consumer's expense is the new normal.

Consumer confidence in corporations lingers at an all-time low, unless they dazzle with a popular consumer device or new, tailor-made benefit to us. Even then, the seduction is short lived. The most profitable technology company whose "designed in California" products are made with low-wages in China, are so well known for litigious enforcement of their image as well as patent filing and litigation, that I won't name them. Through creative strategies, they avoid paying taxes on billions in taxable income yearly by hiding profits in foreign countries, regardless that they define themselves as an American enterprise, and they are not alone. The average person sees more easily and frequently the discrepancy between professed corporate values and actual actions.

Consumers struggle with a deep mistrust of companies and their brands. Shrewd investors wonder if a company in a meteoric rise is simply a bubble about to burst. These practices hurt many traditionally service-based businesses, like your plumber or electrician. It damages the image of business start-ups. When people evaluate a salesperson or a company, they often focus directly on the person and people involved, because the brand and company they represent is no longer trusted. Will this person keep their promises? Although leadership is part of building and maintaining integrity in the marketplace, it goes deeper. Reliable leaders committed to service rise above the pack of habitually two-faced businessmen.

These practices profoundly impact one of the oldest of social rituals, the giving and receiving of goods, the buyer and seller relationship. Attention to the sellers' needs has collapsed under a concentration on the buyers' needs, because of an environment of abundance and customization of goods. Features and benefits matter little—nothing said convinces a buyer anymore.

It has become a market all about what, when, and where the buyer needs something, anything. The marketplace bows down to the god of "all about them." In this business atmosphere, the best way to gain customer loyalty is through publicly displayed values, your professional integrity. This also applies to personal integrity, because they are one and the same. You can't fake integrity because it's part of your identity. A plumber, an electrician, a father, husband, wife; while these incorporate identity, they also exist as roles worn like a familiar coat.

Integrity resists simulation. It isn't a want, it's a need. Unless you are too big to fail, without it, you'll be unable to sustain your service to others. Commitment to integrity grounds and supports everything, and emerges through leadership by example.

The information age has yielded to partnership, collaboration, respect and mutual service. Information lacks its former power of currency because it's free, accessible to all. How-to books and posts fill the internet for most any task imaginable. Do It Yourself (DIY) instruction exists in varied and endless forms. However, with easy access, it's now become obvious that *not everyone* has the ability to DIY for every task and do it well.

Once I attempted plumbing on my girlfriend's condo with disastrous results. I now avoid attempts to weld pipes together with no experience beyond an internet video. The value of ideas has plummeted because everyone has an opinion. However, implementation remains important because skills acquired from experience and knowing their worth are equally valuable. I learned that the hard way from leaky pipes. Doing instead of talking sets people apart, but doing things well pushes you to the front of the race.

The increased pace of change and customization has accelerated an obvious survival-of- the-fittest Darwin-like environment. In nature, dependent organisms, parasites, and the somewhat independent organisms, lone wolves, evolve slower and die faster in a rapidly changing environment. Market pressure has become corrupted at an accelerated rate, like a corked bottle with an increasing fermented gas build-up, exploding in economic recessions.

Honest business people, willing to acknowledge their weaknesses and strengths, plan to maintain good relationships. They realize they can't do everything on their own and need a compass for this storm. They grasp their carefully considered core values and a public code of conduct in order to survive. Reacting isn't enough; you must be proactive. Define what you stand for and stay true to yourself despite ongoing struggles.

Integrity is more than survival. It holds positive benefits for everyone, even though survival remains important the midst of critical change. Integrity clarifies your life's meaning. It accelerates gains in your personal and professional life and through instant power, greater creativity and freedom.

Trust enhances all of these. Your partners, colleagues and friends rely on you because they know your uncompromising stand for people and principles no matter the pressure. Your employees know you'll back them; your customers know you understand their business and will take care of them. They recognize your integrity which allows you to display of tailor-made quality and service. You earn this through intentional cultivation of character.

You can't fake integrity because it's part of your identity.

#IntegrityBook #Integrity

PART III:
CHALLENGE OF DEFINING
INTEGRITY

Think for a moment. What does integrity mean? Although you may name a few common characteristics, try to define it so well that that you answer all possible questions about it. Any attempt to be clear and without debate proves very hard. Trying to thoroughly define it revealed many contradictions. For example, honesty is similar to integrity, and people with integrity are also generally honest.

However, if you are honest about your evil choices, is that integrity? You could choose to follow a corrupt man who is forthright about his wickedness, or a *good man*, like an anonymous donor, who conceals his beneficial actions for others and society. Does integrity insure full compliance with the law? Many non-Nazi soldiers in the German army during World War II were given orders to murder civilians. Did those who disobeyed their orders lack integrity?

I'm told I have it, but I struggle to identify and quantify it. Although I referred to a dictionary, and read anything I could find on the subject, the definition eluded me. Many people think about it. A popular online dictionary reports the word "integrity" is in the top 1% of words looked up and is the 24th most popular English word in the world.

Integrity's impact goes beyond being a valuable personal trait—it's critical for exemplary business policies and transactions. Research indicates that integrity generally describes character and behavior driven by certain values. However, using this definition, these values might be misunderstood, or seen as "correct" or "right" by an individual and then applied to harm others. A monster, acting in accordance with *his* values, would perpetrate evil toward others. Consider racism and hate from multiple cultural perspectives. In 1991 I was probably attacked because I looked like a homosexual; I was different from the accepted norm in my community. Remember your own experiences.

Although Americans love the word, it's rare to find individuals who have it or know what it means. Its frequent use in politics erodes its importance because this is an arena where people rarely do what they say or say what they mean. Widespread misuse of the word creates confusion. Despite nostalgic associations with our past, like segments of religion and culture, its once-clear definition has fragmented into various mythologies.

Against this backdrop, care becomes essential in defining it, simply because integrity is an unquestioned and undefined ideal people attach to morality. That connection indicates the potential for extreme subjectivity. In addition, determining who has this quality becomes open to interpretation. Looking back, the love of the ideal and its wide usage runs deep through our American history and identity.

Dictionary definitions abound. One is wholeness, which applied to an individual means "being consistent or congruent in their manner." Another one says, "…as having the same size and shape…" or matching with something. What do these definitions mean? A person of integrity acts and behaves in a way in which is generally the same; regardless of person or circumstance…or someone who does not say opposing or different things to different people to gain their approval or trust. Integrity excludes deceit, insincerity, and hypocrisy. It includes wholeness, singularity and perfection. A person of integrity strictly abides by a code of high moral values.

I own a company that designs and creates custom software solutions for businesses. The software and Information Technology world has its own use of the word. When describing information storage structures on computers called databases, the word also has a particular definition and meaning.

A database is a collection of data, or information, organized for use on a computer. It's basically a list with each item called "data", like a filing cabinet with each folder in the cabinet called data instead of a file. These lists can get highly complex. For example, they can store all of the product entries of an online shopping website (and then some), and can be made of multiple databases. This is the general idea. Within this very technical and functional way to store and access data, reliability is critical. This is where integrity comes in.

Database "integrity" refers to the care and responsibility for the accuracy and consistency of the data. It encompasses all the maintenance and management of the information, and is part of its design, configuration, and use. Integrity means strict adherence to a "code" like the ability of the information storage to observe the rules in a way that prevents loss or corruption of the material.

How would you feel if your spouse gave you a shopping list that was unreadable with the words blurred by water? What if half was missing, torn off, and you only realized this when you got home? Frustrated, you'd need to make multiple trips to the store or explain why you didn't buy your spouse's favorite shampoo. This example illustrates the crisis of corrupted data. Very scary.

This is why database integrity receives extraordinary attention by excellent engineers and why the rules and the discipline itself demand extreme care in creation. The displacement of items on that list or false and unreadable items can cost a business millions of dollars in losses. Thus backups, or archived copies, are made to ensure recovery.

Some people might wish we could clone politicians and replace them with earlier, less corrupt versions with little downtime to our government, in the same way we often can with databases in computing. Instead, society has ineffectual penalties that fail to thoroughly fix this, instead of applying stronger measures like—disgrace, lost status and prison.

In summary, the word integrity has various vague, often personal and idealistic interpretations, especially when applied to a person's nature or character.

I narrow the definitions to:

- a description applied to one's character, referencing a pattern of behavior, driven by certain values (so that it can be understood and applied to business practices)
- one who acts and behaves in a way in which is generally the same regardless of person or circumstance, or someone who does not say things to different people to gain their approval or trust, who abides by values
- one free of deceit, insincerity and hypocrisy
- one who strictly abides by a code of high moral values
- accuracy or consistency to the rules
- a lack of corruption or loss

Comparing these definitions to my experiences reveals a pattern and confirms the importance of integrity. Selecting specific rules is a personal choice best served when targeting self-improvement. Belief systems determine correct choices with the focus on personal leadership through actions, rather than one-upmanship designed to flaunt your superiority.

Invest deliberate concern and careful thought in delineating what is right and wrong. Your deeds become examples to ignore, follow, or react against. Have the confidence to act publicly even if later it costs or humiliates you. Your behavior holds you accountable; you're not just talking for the sake of being heard, or performing to be seen.

A person with integrity strives for

i. A personal focus to modify his behavior as an example to others, making consistent and public efforts to act with understanding.

ii. Deliberate investment and careful thought into what is right and wrong.

iii. Doing what he promises, even at a personal cost.

DOING WHAT YOU SAY YOU WILL DO

It is universally agreed that people with integrity have actions that match their promises. A good start is observable behavior, worthy of respect. Action exhibits many characteristics of integrity. Public displays of values, reliability, and commitment with follow through demonstrate it. Sadly, many people make promises and never deliver. A common saying regarding home repair people is, "if you want to be successful, show up." Merely doing what you say you will do demonstrates remarkable behavior.

I grew up in Florida, the first state to have the horse *and* the cow. Florida is called *cracker* country, a term of respect and also a slur for poor white people not unlike the word *redneck*. *Cracker* first surfaced in the Middle English period between the twelfth and fifteenth centuries. It originated with the word crack, meaning "entertaining conversation", and retains that meaning in Ireland, Scotland and parts of England in the form of "craic". At one point in history it described braggarts. Despite that, ultimately, this history imparts importance and cultural dignity to the word.

Florida has its own version of cowboy, a term historically applied to those who worked with and drove cattle and other livestock. They differed from the Western cowboys or Spanish "*vaqueros*". We called them "cowmen", "cow hunters", or "crackers". During the 1800's most of a cow hunter's time was spent locating his herd or strays in the unfenced flat scrub and woodlands. The Florida folk meaning for cracker connected the term to the sharp noise of the whip, unlike the lasso of the Western cowboy. Traditional westerns and cowboy movies display a huge sky above open expanses of land, a logical place to see and lasso cattle. The lasso required room to maneuver and time to get the rope swinging enough to control a whirling loop aimed at a wayward cow's neck.

Dogs, like the working mutt, the "Florida black-mouthed cur," are bred and trained to find grazing cattle and to instinctively group them in a herd, so that the whip can drive them. The faithful dog from the Disney movie Old Yeller was the most famous of these frontier dogs. I was lucky enough to raise one of these hardy and tough dogs, named "Seamus" (an

Irish name pronounced *SHAY-mus*) for the whole of his life, about 10 years.

Florida lacked expansive plains. Tropical rainfall and heat produced thick stands of trees and plants. Unlike northern forests with tall trees and only a few plants at their base which permitted easy mobility, all Florida ground is choked with vegetation in endless competition for sunlight and rainwater. This environment favored a different breed of cattle, smaller, tougher, with larger horns and larger feet. These animals could handle the tough, treacherous ground which shifted from powdery sand to marsh.

In Florida the lasso was useless. Cow hunters learned that whips and dogs worked better. The *crack* of the whip, combined with the respected preference for good storytelling and entertaining conversation during long work days, made the term *cracker* synonymous with the *cow hunter*, and became a popular term to describe them.

For a time *cracker* was used as an insult to the huge migration of poor white natives, new residents to Florida. Using it was a good way to start a fight. Now Floridians romanticize it to describe a culture different from the tourists brought to the state by Disney, the invention of air conditioning, mosquito repellant and window screens. Its use evokes nostalgia and pride about a time and culture that was formerly dominant, but is now confined to the country, where tourists rarely go, blue collar work workers live, and old Florida attractions remain.

My grandfather came to Florida to help start a pre-Disney attraction called Cypress Gardens, now extinct and transformed into Legoland. I was raised in this culture which gave grave importance to doing what you say you would do, or *giving your word*, often sealed simply by a handshake.

This is only one aspect of a culture that established itself on family, ethics, truth, honesty, and strength of character, respect and living with nature, animals and the land. Old Westerns celebrated these things. Today the mark of Florida is beaches and Disney.

Being a person of your word is so well respected and enforced that being seen as someone "whose word is no good" makes you a social outcast, untrustworthy and weak. These values were handed down from parents to children and seriously enforced by parents and grandparents. Your character elicits respect; unreliability diminishes your worth. The glue of cherished values held a hardworking people together and kept them strong in the face of adversity.

People are shocked to discover that Florida cattlemen still trade cattle and land in multi-million dollar deals with people in faraway states on nothing more than a handshake, leaving attorneys left behind to document the transactions. Bringing up a contract to sign is still considered an insult. A piece of paper is worthless to people who trade based fully on character and proven commitment to fulfilling their word.

Developing this quality is easy in theory, yet hard in practice. On a day-to-day basis, treat large and small commitments as inviolable, no matter the consequences. Reject failure as an option and consider every obligation a very serious thing, remembering even trivial promises. Establish the perception by choice that you value people, commitments and your own character. Let others know that they can *always* count on you.

On a day-to-day basis, treat large and small commitments as inviolable, no matter the consequences.

#IntegrityBook #Integrity

SCRUTINY

Careful consideration forms the core of developing integrity, simultaneously a skill and asset. Over time your ideas and decisions that print out the currency of your future. To amass character wealth, analyze your experiences, rather than operating from reactive instincts. Continue by applying your knowledge of the past to serve as a tool, so that you can recognize and appropriate transformative opportunities, as well as to avoid pitfalls others fail to see.

Because change is constant, intentionally exercise judgment. You can't draw a conclusion after careful thought and then shelve it until you need it again. Regular review of your principles hones your ability to see differences and similarities in situations and construct new decisions from past reasoning and experiences. A review of history shows that change in individuals and society shifts the perception of right and wrong. Although dramatic change is infrequent, it occurs.

For example, significant development in society includes adjustments in the recognized standards of right and wrong. Behavior considered right today may be wrong tomorrow for logical, moral, or religious reasons such as the opinions on slavery, woman's rights, and even human sacrifice which have changed throughout the course of history. Accepted mores centuries ago in Rome differ greatly from today. Seemingly inviolable ideals vary with time, culture, and between individuals. Living by well-constructed principles and leading by example shows consideration and respect for others.

This demonstrates the need for prudent evaluation of all factors available before making choices. Ethical considerations don't have to be an *untested* basis in your own beliefs or the blindly followed beliefs of others. However, danger comes with choosing life standards based only on your beliefs. Clarify the meaning and motivations of why and what you believe by exploration, inquiry and consideration in real-life situations. Bring good questions to bear not only on hypothetical possibilities, but also on yourself. Why do you behave as you do? Why do you believe certain things? An analytical mind is your greatest tool for developing integrity.

Whole, congruent people commit to authentic displays of inner convictions, while permitting regular re-evaluation of their core beliefs. An individual's integrity should reveal on the public stage of life, the same person seen offstage. Transparency and consistency fuel a fully embraced, simplified life and the ability to make decisions without doubt or hesitation. Authentic people live out their beliefs.

An unlived belief proves to be mere philosophy or theory, thought for thinking's sake alone, without practical application. Unquestioned belief proves to be like insubstantial sand under the pounding waves of reality. Yet people everywhere hold unquestioned beliefs they were raised with; this is normal. The extreme practice of brainwashing limits internal and external wholeness; it prohibits people from questioning and rigidly conditions them to embrace certain tenets.

An untested belief I held was, "trust is not something easily earned." I don't recall where it came from, possibly absorbed from my early school environment. I thought I couldn't trust others unless they expended great effort to earn it. In turn, I applied this to myself—I believed I had to gain others' faith in me through extreme exertion which resulted in awkward situations. People would trust me and I'd behave as if they shouldn't... yet. I thought I hadn't adequately proven myself. I was so focused on my beliefs about the situation that I failed to consider others. My perception blocked my ability to see reality.

On the other hand, unexamined beliefs don't

negate integrity, but unraveling them helps develop life principles. Striving, questioning, and continuous analysis solidify integrity.

In third grade I attended a private Christian school because they provided free tuition through their low-income outreach. (The excellent education showed when I returned to public school for fourth grade, noticeably ahead of the other students.) Our classroom was arranged in a "C" shape, with the teacher's desk in the open end of the "C".

One teacher gave me a bad feeling from the beginning—I never trusted her; she never earned it. Sarcasm and fake smiles permeated her comments. Her words left the impression of hidden intent, somehow wrong, even though her delivery was carefully polished. Even as a child, my gut said "beware." She seemed trapped doing something she didn't want to do, but pretending she did. Grown-ups talked about her as an outsider, a disliked other. I still remember her name. Despite my feeling, I behaved in her class and tried to enjoy myself. After all, she may have had unseen burdens that made her that way.

One afternoon during a particularly long lecture, the student to my immediate left raised his hand. She often ignored raised hands until she finished. Her unresponsiveness conveyed the message that she simply wasn't going to acknowledge him. I forgot about him and focused on the lesson.

Sometime later he started shaking. I could feel it through the table. He had his head down on one arm, the other hand still up. I stared, wondering why he trembled, and then returned to my book when I couldn't figure it out. A few minutes passed. I heard a sniffle, an almost silent whine like a dog in pain. This continued every few minutes for a long time until he had my full attention. I decided to risk trouble by asking him what was going on; he still had his hand up and was behaving strangely. I waited for an opportunity. Maybe the teacher would turn away. I looked back and forth between him and the teacher.

My moving head caught her attention. I felt cold inside as her penetrating eyes targeted me. She noticed him as well, although her false expression indicated her deep interest in her lecture. I thought I might be in trouble, like I'd been caught doing something I shouldn't.

At this point the student peeked at her and realized I was watching him. His look screamed silent anguish. His face was purple, red, and white, wet with tears of pain and humiliation, despite his effort to choke them back, and avoid calling attention to himself with his hand still up. Fear quaked inside me. The table started shaking again.

I studied him more closely and realized he wasn't actually sitting in his chair. He was crouched, with his upper body in a sitting pose, his legs awkwardly bent in a stress position. He'd probably been this way for quite a while, standing strangely like that and trying to hide his crying. Urine had pooled in his seat and saturated his pants, legs, socks, and shoes. It puddled beneath him. Waiting to be acknowledged and avoid tremendous embarrassment had left him trying to hide his humiliation.

Two things struck me. He'd been crouching for a long time. The puddle on the floor was dried around the edges. The teacher would have seen this happen, because she had a clear view below our table.

She ignored him on purpose.

I knew this was wrong and imagined his deep physical and emotional pain. Anger swelled inside me. My parents constantly taught me to know the difference between right and wrong and instructed me to do the right thing. They expected me to be honest and forthright, even if it hurt, because deceit was wrong. Being caught in dishonesty later would hurt much, much worse.

My dad's actions and words taught me to protect the weak and disadvantaged like a warrior. He wanted me to imitate his strength and conviction, because he said few fight for the disadvantaged, or for the right and the good. My mother instructed me as a caregiver and registered nurse, helping the sick and giving fully of herself to heal others' pain.

In my eyes that teacher became the enemy and from then on I viewed her with careful, constant suspicion. I communicated this to her with a stare of intense disapproval, the best I could do with my little round face and bowl haircut. There was no doubt *she* knew that *I* knew what she had done. She immediately sent him to the bathroom and then left the room to get the janitor. The whole class looked around suddenly for she rarely stopped a lecture like this, ever. Her class was a marathon of impulse control under deliberate instruction.

I told my parents that afternoon. Much drama followed among the adults with phone calls, discussion, and disbelief. I learned from my mother that the student had bladder problems, and the school had a doctor's note that gave him special permission to go to the restroom *anytime* he needed to. This teacher added one condition – he had to ask first. However, she ignored his silent, appropriate request because it appeared she believed her lecture was more important.

Subsequently, I dissected her behavior and motives. She knew I'd told the adults what had happened because I was named as a witness. I don't believe that she claimed I was lying, although afterward she acted differently around me. I didn't get special treatment, either good or bad. She understood that I was aware of the adult world and how it worked. Perhaps she realized I was scrutinizing her motivations as well as her actions. From thereon I viewed her as the "Bad Teacher."

HONESTY

Honest people don't manipulate the truth by showcasing some facts and omitting others. Truthful individuals demonstrate transparency, making it apparent they have the best interests of others in mind. At times candor involves risk, in providing complete service to others, as well as standing up for beliefs or admitting to faults. Honest people display vulnerability, even in threatening circumstances, accepting the consequences of potential or certain punishment. Vulnerability displays great strength, not weakness; only the strong can choose it.

Without tact, honesty is self-serving; without consideration for the effect of words on others; it's like a thin veneer of the real trait flaunted for your own pleasure, a lazy stance. Genuine contemplation about the impact of truthful remarks prompts extra effort to assure that they'll be well received.

Sensitivity and discretion make honesty courteous for those challenging situations handled tactfully. Consideration often elicits admiration. Decisions made in a logical way can be delivered as nurturing or as mentoring advice. Keeping the relationship foremost, rather than seeking to persuade or gain an advantage, indicates a clear and forthright giver, not a deceptive taker.

I was taught about BB guns as a young teen. I understood their power through shootouts with guns borrowed from my cousins, but didn't learn about responsibility until I actually owned one. When my cousins and I used them on each other and the neighborhood kids while playing around, it hurt. They probably still have scars or a BB underneath their skin. One cousin was left unsupervised for long periods of time, while his parents worked and were seldom home. We got into lots of trouble with BB guns.

Once he put a raccoon skin hat on, gave me a matching one and we went out "hunting." He shot a dove or a pigeon in the neighborhood and we took it to his house. He de-feathered it in the garage, gutted it, and said he was going to roast and eat it. I got the hell out of there, because I was afraid he was going to make me eat that nasty bird. He was a little older than me with unpredictable behavior.

When I got my own BB gun, my parents told me

only to play with it when they were home, and always shoot it with the barrel pointed at the ground. Being young and having that kind of exciting toy around, I disobeyed them. One day I went out to shoot stuff— lizards and birds, whatever. I was in the back yard and a butterfly came into view, a perfect bright colored target. I aimed high and fired without thinking about what might be behind it. I was too focused on my target and too young to think that this wasn't a good idea with nearby neighbors.

I pulled the trigger. Instantly it hit something hard on the neighbor's side of the bushes. I'd missed the butterfly. My heart froze, wondering what I'd struck. My life lessons often came the first time I did something stupid.

I ran around the bush and stopped in horror at the sight of a broken window. I began crying. It was obvious what I should and shouldn't have been doing. Afraid, I ran inside and hid to think because my parents weren't home. I spun out a scenario. The neighbors would find the broken window, suspect a break-in and wonder if anything had been stolen. They would be worried, feel violated. If the police got involved and alerted the whole neighborhood, they'd be looking for a thief in hiding, uneasy that it might be someone they knew. I had to tell that neighbor before everything unraveled, especially before my parents found out.

I left the house carrying my BB gun as evidence, and started around the block to the neighbor's house.

It seemed like I was pushing against a very strong wind, trudging to my own execution, but I kept putting one foot in front of the other. I started crying again. Then I stood in front of the door and knocked. There was no answer.

Panic began. What if they weren't home and everything I'd imagined happened before I could stop it? I started pounding on the door, yelling "Hello," so loudly that someone in their back yard could have heard me.

Suddenly the door opened and I stood facing the man of the house. He spoke in such a kind way that I felt even more terrible. "Can I help you?"

I wanted to look down, or away, anywhere but at him. "I'm sorry, but I broke your window. I shot it with this BB gun." I held it out as evidence.

"Well, that's funny because I didn't hear any windows break. That's okay. We'll fix it and you can have your parents pay us for it."

I felt relief for confessing, but trepidation that my dad would find out I had disobeyed him. I told him in great detail about the butterfly; how I shot it, that the window broke, that I lived behind him, and every unnecessary detail I could think of. Explaining felt so good that I couldn't stop. I thought I could talk my way out of trouble, crying the whole time.

"Wait a minute; you're kid that lives behind us?"

"Yes, sir."

"Let's go take a look." He led the way to the back yard and pointed. "You mean this window?"

"Yes, sir." I shook inside.

"It was already broken. That's why we put the wooden board behind it. "

The hole was too large for a BB, and some care had been taken to plug it. Disbelief filled me.

The man walked around inspecting the other windows. None were broken. He returned to the spot where I stood. "Thank you for being honest, but no damage was done. Just be careful with that thing little man, and always point it at the ground."

Sometimes verbal lessons need to be repeated.

Vulnerability displays great strength, not weakness; only the strong can choose it.

#IntegrityBook #Integrity

QUESTIONING

No one knows everything. Asking questions can be hard, but inquiry is critical to developing integrity. Questions admit a lack of knowledge and willingness to learn. Why would people want or need to read a book, if they already knew it all?

Questioning yourself and others should be accepted and natural, especially when keeping those in authority accountable. People are living books, because each person has a story worth telling, something to contribute to others. Queries and answers increase understanding of the strengths and limitations of yourself and others. Even formulating questions stimulates knowledge and wisdom. Inquiry knits relationships together as you learn about what others know and believe. People provide the opportunity to converse and analyze, which is something unavailable from mere words on a page.

They offer unique viewpoints. Their singular and complex insights provide more connection than you can glean from simply reading.

Information from books and videos is like a simple meal for your senses. By comparison, the multi-dimensional communication of shared stories provides a feast. It's like a meal with an appetizer, a main course, a dessert and a perfectly paired drink. Carefully chosen words, intonation, and pace combine with body language and emotion to convey more meaning, fuller answers.

No personal disadvantages come from asking questions—no *personal disadvantages*. Others *may* perceive an attitude of mistrust, or be authorities unaccustomed to being quizzed. Some people discourage inquiry under a pretense of respect saying, "It's not appropriate to ask questions." Even if direct inquiries are thwarted, you can maintain mental analysis, and apply it more forcefully when answers are clearly withheld.

An inquiring mind isn't a disobedient or disrespectful mind. When committed to following orders, such as those from superiors in a corporation, questioning doesn't imply or approve disobedience as long as you are thoughtful about the timing and have demonstrated a willingness to obey. It acknowledges you desire more information which you've not yet received. Your questions signify you want greater understanding, not to create friction or demonstrate a disrespectful disobedience.

Curiosity marks childhood. Everything is new and daily discoveries fuel the desire to learn. As children get older some questions meet disapproval or resistance, especially if the person asked doesn't know or was afraid to appear ignorant, especially in education or religion.

Perhaps questioning ended when answers were handed to you. Much school instruction revolves around question-killing answers. Information is presented in a way designed to discourage further inquiry. "Two plus two is four." Why is it four? Who invented math? I know because I asked and found out the answers.

It's time to ask questions again and revive youthful curiosity. You can employ your more educated mind to broaden your knowledge and increase your wisdom.

Did you stop asking because you didn't want to know, feared the answer or were simply frustrated in the search? Apprehension comes from unexpected or unpleasant answers. Everyone experiences this.

Life isn't always fair. Good people get bad answers in the same way that bad things sometimes happen to good people. Nevertheless every situation offers an opportunity to grow. Some of the most significant lessons come from adverse things. Each day contains tailor-made meaning, even in distasteful and undesirable moments.

Access the power of reflection. Then true motivations will surface; honest self-examination reveals why you do the things you do. That knowledge forms the platform for constructive change. Out of this kind of intentional process you'll equip yourself to make better decisions. Not only will creativity increase, but your critical thinking will sharpen. You'll better define what you know and don't know about subjects that matter to you. You'll accelerate the acquisition of new ideas and sources of information.

With practice, the quality of information you derive from your inquiries will improve. Better questions will emerge because you know who, where, when, and why to ask them. Ultimately, all answers are driven by questions.

Memorization and participation differ. School instruction often only requires the memorization of facts or simple ways of connecting them. Although star students, usually fantastic memorizers, make top marks on tests, their skill differs from critical thinking which requires an engaged mind.

Asking questions creates the quickest way to engage the mind. Try asking a question for every statement. For example, "The fastest way to engage a mind is by asking questions." The answer is, "What is the fastest way to engage the mind when presented with a fact?"

Socrates, a Greek philosopher (470/469 BC – 399 BC), considered one of the founders of Western philosophy, contributed much to the exploration of ethical matters. He used a unique teaching style. He asked questions that led the student to consider and comprehend the foundations of what was being said and develop more refined thinking patterns. All answers were connected and supported by other thoughts, beliefs and answers like a spider's web.

This style of learning by asking questions prompted broader understanding of any issue by looking at it from every possible direction. Instead of just seeing the spider or the web, you could observe the beauty of the pattern and evidence of the wind as it blew through the strands and made the web dance. Answers contain agendas, desires that bring it into being. By understanding these motivations, you grasp more fully facts, beliefs, desires, or any type of information. You begin to feel the wind.

People are living books, because each person has a story worth telling, something to contribute to others.

#IntegrityBook #Integrity

STUBBORN VS STEADFAST

Defined ideologies enable people to persevere in the face of obstacles and difficulties. While some ingrained beliefs only change after lengthy consideration, adherence to convictions upholds strong beliefs as well as integrity. A considered and intentional shift can be good, not merely a sudden collapse in the midst of adversity. Resolute individuals hold fast to solid principles, resisting corruption. Moral instability reveals self-centered and unreliable character; we distrust those who flip positions and policies in order to impress or gain favor; their weak character dissuades loyal followers. Their quoted words evoke ridicule rather than admiration.

Without meaningful direction in life, perseverance rests on the luck of the ignorant, or extreme and zealous behavior. Knowing why hardships come makes that burden bearable. Meaning derived from enduring adversity or even facing down and surviving death, strengthens the ability to enthusiastically thrive in the best of times.

Perseverance risks becoming stubbornness without the wisdom of designing thoughtfully designed strategies for change. Appropriate discernment requires openness to new positions, possibilities, and viewpoints. Ignoring them and failing to take the time to examine them, isn't steadfastness, but stubbornness, a deliberate, willful ignorance. This fearful reaction has roots in lazy self-deception.

Sustained integrity demands continuous effort. But even those with well-developed integrity can fall into the trap of inflexibility from stress, lack of effort, or unidentified, insidious bad habits.

Within weeks of being laid off during the first major recession in 2001, I put together a team on a new project and continued with what I had been doing in the corporate world, but now I was my own boss. I knew little about business or working for clients, for I was an employee only six years before striking out on my own. Years passed before I gained that knowledge, although I was surrounded by people quick to offer opinions and advice, which I rarely took.

I thought that few people understood technical work, but I should have been willing to listen. After four years as a freelancer, I agreed that I should have a "company" legally created for my protection and for tax purposes. Immediately the same advice–wielding people told me how to structure it. I felt like a bachelor with parental pressure to marry and then fresh pressure to produce children as soon as the wedding vows had been exchanged.

Years later we got a financial and legal team in place, and restructured our company. My financial team was a little horrified with my procedures; according to them, I was paying too much in taxes. Previously, I'd used a professional firm to process my businesses taxes, and said, "Have me pay if there's any question at all." I joked about being a patriot, when in reality, I was simply stubborn.

I never understood taxes or tax laws beyond the necessity of complying, and didn't consider it important, so I paid more than my share. Money didn't motivate me, nor was I suspicious or hate-filled toward the government. I'd never been harassed, believed I understood authority, and was okay with taxation. The government uses laws and guidelines to communicate its rules. However, there are some breaks the government allows which reduces the amount paid, and I didn't take them.

I grew up with computers. They were everywhere—businesses, schools, banks, companies, utility facilities and so on. I couldn't comprehend that the Internal Revenue Service was less computerized than I was. Until recent history, they continued to do things the old-fashioned way, relying on simple manpower and paper reviews to discover cheats.

I also didn't know that most inquiries they had were limited to people asking questions during an audit. How many people live in this nation? Then how many people are necessary to competently review everyone's taxes? The comparison defies comprehension. Had I decided to cheat (which I didn't), I'd fear doing it, assuming incorrectly that giant math computers ran the IRS which would instantly identify my fraudulent submission.

My excuse was that I was too busy having fun in my new career, building a business and flying around the world to force myself to understand it. Because I wasn't inclined to cheat, I was okay with giving the government more than most people believed it deserved. However, I knew I should look into it; people had raised questions that remained unanswered, but my resistance persisted.

Now, I implement a process called "triangulation" to combat any tendencies toward lazy thinking. If I get the same advice from more than two or three people, I know I must investigate, not taking potential life changes lightly. Once I select key items, I address them with the full focus of my faculties. Only then can I extract the greatest information and wisdom, to ensure certainty about the decisions I make. Those who know me best generally offer the best advice. After I wait to hear the same thing from two more people, and then investigate, my wife often says, "You could shortcut the process and just listen to me the first time."

PART IV:
BENEFITS FOR YOURSELF

Many benefits accrue from clarifying what you believe and what you represent. This enhances confidence in yourself and your choices, slashing time spent making decisions because you know yourself and have established priorities. Decisions flow and doubts diminish as you build your future achievements on the foundation of integrity.

Regular personal reflection brings rewards. Looking inward decreases anxiety and releases the bondage of desperate desire for approval or acceptance. Self-reliance and independence free you to choose partnerships and associations rather than remain linked to others out of need. Operating from options to choose rather than desperation transforms relationships, opening the way for equality and a mutual exchange of time and energy.

Planning the future becomes easier when you've spent the time to review where you've been and considered where you want to go. This doesn't mean you can be sure of every detail, but you gain an advantage over those who are clueless and unfocused.

In the absence of precise long-term dreams, you still hold the tools needed to accomplish short-term goals. Discipline and constructive behavior enable you to create a plan, follow through, and achieve your short term goals with greater success. Your will directs your success rather than luck. Consistently achieving short term goals sets the stage for accomplishing long-term ones.

Success needs to be repeatable for long-term transformation. Without integrity, you lean on chance. Integrity underlies dependable behavior and, thus, achievement. In our "win-the-lottery-and-live-it-up" culture, many people waste time seeking short-term fixes, or searching for a shortcut to the big prize. It's like limiting nutrition to a bite of an appetizer or a dish of dessert, neglecting the most important part— the actual meal. The abbreviated outlook gives the same result as quick strategies by focusing on the vision and dream alone without doing the necessary work. Skipping the critical part of nutrition diminishes strength and stamina. In the same way, short-sighted choices cripple character.

You can achieve in spite of yourself, if you have the right behavior. Most of my life I was surprised by my accomplishments, because I was all behavior. For example, if I was asked to dig a large hole, I would gladly pick up a shovel and start digging without noticing that the shovel was leaning on a bulldozer.

I simply had no goals and no vision.

As a consultant, I helped others realize their dreams and create an overall vision and plan, but failed to do this for myself.

Most people gladly share their dreams, but equally often, those dreamers fail to achieve, because their dreaming supplanted actual work. At the core they were weak and lazy. I wanted to be different and tell stories about what I had actually done.

Accomplishments, not dreams, define you. I mistakenly concluded dreaming was worthless, and gained happiness and excitement from what I created and acquired. I was very sensitive about discussing my goals. If I told a friend about where I wanted to be three times, or complained three times, I'd get angry and resolve to act immediately. Doing versus talking became my highest and most immediate priority. Dreaming, fantasy, vacation and escape can be creative, healthy, and constructive; but only if they have purpose—to help you in a constructive way.

Two things matter: what you do and the people you love. Your relationships gain depth and dependability when you have a life of integrity. Solid connections are available in business as well, especially in a service-based industry. Even less service-based professions contain a relationship component because all business operates upon the exchange of something of value. With the close of the information age, your sales message, your marketing, and what you say is less important than what you do, and whether you keep your promises.

Integrity underlies dependable behavior and, thus, achievement.

#IntegrityBook #Integrity

SELF-EXAMINATION

It takes time and effort to make the correct choice, choose the right path, and properly judge a situation or someone's character. Over time you can learn to distinguish the disparity between motivations and actions. Although someone might express a desire to do something, his actions may be contrary to his words.

The ability to sort out right and wrong has great value in criminal trials. When evaluating character, which is of greater importance, intentions or actions? How do actions reveal intentions? Can valid judgment be rendered without the proper time and effort to consider these things?

The following story illustrates the difference between motivations and actions. A witness observes two characters, a Judge and an Executioner. Consider their roles. If you had to pick one of the two roles for a day, which would you want?

A judge listens, evaluates and makes weighty decisions. In some cases, he can overrule a jury and impose his will on the accused. He holds the power of life and death. If he condemns someone to death, does that mar his character? He pronounces consequences following appropriate consideration. If you held his position, think about how your choices would affect others.

Often a jury helps, but not all trials are jury trials. The verdict and sentence affects the life of the condemned, the lives of others, and the future. The judge's burden is to live with the consequences.

So would you choose to be the judge? Most prefer this, because the executioner has to kill someone. He's the one with blood on his hands; he carries out death sentences. This job may conflict with your religious beliefs.

In addition, the justice system isn't perfect; today DNA evidence sometimes vindicates innocent people on death row. Then after decades of an impending execution, the system declares its mistake and sets the prisoner free. Before DNA exoneration, an innocent man could be executed. However, if that information comes too late, the executioner has shut the door on his release. Compliance with orders provides little comfort; executioners aren't tasked to determine innocence or guilt. The judge's sentence holds whether or not his peers or public opinion concurs.

On the other hand, an executioner's refusal to carry out a death sentence simply passes the job on to a willing executioner. The death sentence will be carried out with or without the reluctant executioner; the condemned will die. Consider how you would approach his task. Analyze your intentions. Think about all of the aspects of the commitment.

Now imagine you're a witness. When you go to watch the execution you observe the judge gleefully rubbing his hands. In contrast, the executioner takes great care to make ensure the condemned is comfortable and respected; he takes every precaution for a swift death with minimal suffering.

As the witness, who appears to harbor evil intentions? Who shows greater integrity? In the end, who bears the greater responsibility for the outcome?

I first heard this story when I was sixteen. It gripped my heart and mind because it contained an important truth—these of roles all exist inside of me. They represent the different perspectives of my mind by which I interpret my external reality.

Throughout my life, the judge in me weighs outcomes and makes endless rounds of decisions. My imagination draws the past into my present and projects images of my yet-to-exist future. However, memories are imperfect copies; each one contains little twists colored by interpretation.

Detectives wish witnesses had perfect recall, but reality proves accounts of events are not only incomplete but differ greatly from one person to another. A video from a well-known study demonstrates the mind's ability to filter reality. A basketball team passes the ball, and the observer is instructed to count the number of times it changes hands. Most people simply do not see the man in the gorilla suit dancing through the scene.

The executioner in me carries out my decisions. Thank goodness, only a few people have the actual job of executioner. The root of the word "executioner" is "execute" and means "to do." The extended definition is, "to do something that you have planned to do, or you have been told to do". A similar, but less sinister word, "executor," means "someone who is responsible for executing, or following through, on an assigned task or duty". The executor in me takes actions based on my judgments.

The witness in me remembers. It observes the judge and the executioner, and the outcome of their decisions and actions. It scrutinizes patterns in my life, and projects short and long-term outcomes. This role bears the weight of interpreting the courtroom drama. It reflects on the incident, the evidence, and the reasoning which produced the verdict and sentence. In life it can effect change by participation, such as how future trials are conducted. In that way, the witness can alter future events and outcomes.

These roles are all part of me. I witness my choices and my response to them. Sometimes unusual outcomes occur, but generally, the results fulfill my desired intentions. If I perceive my world as one full of fear, pain, and evil, I'll act accordingly, and experience the same. This kind of negative outlook affected me when I was a younger man; I viewed life simply in terms of surviving. As a result, I aimed at staying alive, not thriving. In my core, I believed that there had to be a better way, if I could find it – and I kept pursing it.

This story applies to you, even if you don't know it.

You are the judge, the executor or executioner of your own beliefs, and the primary witness to the outcomes. Though you can't control your life challenges, you have the power to limit their effect on you in the future. For instance, two people root for opposing sports teams. One team wins; the other loses. Happiness or unhappiness at the end is based on which team each one supported and their view of the importance of the final score. They chose how the game affected them.

CONDUCT

To form personal standards, you must intentionally determine your moral parameters. Core values can't lead to the life you want if they remain unknown. You must discover who you are and what you represent. In the process of determining these things, remain with the task, in order to avoid compromise. Sense the control and freedom a moral code gives.

Many people view their circumstances as pure chance, products of their environment. An internal dialogue would reveal an image of their life as a leaf on the wind, blown here and there by impersonal whim. But people *aren't* mindless robots, programmed by parents, environment, the system, or even experiences. While circumstances affect your life, they don't fully determine your identity or prevent you from developing integrity. Why? Because you have a choice.

To comprehend the strength of choice, first acknowledge your responsibility for your fate. The blame game ends when you stop faulting others or complaining about circumstances. Here's the hard, but key lesson: results are what you make them. Rewards follow time and effort. That's the system, consistent effort, not instant gratification.

Accepting responsibility is a quality unique to humans. Although animals have similar instincts and behaviors, we can reason and select. For instance, before learning to drive, you may have felt nervous or afraid, even wanting to escape. When animals face danger from predators they are driven by similar instincts and feelings. Yet people have the ability to control the desire to run or scream. You can move toward your fear of driving because you understand the potential rewards. Other challenges, addressed by analysis and experience, enable you to do more than merely survive. You can overcome difficulties rather than be trapped and succumb.

Either you choose or some external force chooses for you. You can press forward to become who you want to be, or commit a critical mistake: make excuses. That deficient response tells the truth: you don't want change badly enough. To progress toward admirable character you must prioritize difficult choices for change.

Many fail to see the reality of their daily choices, because they are blind to their participation; they relinquish their power without resistance. They react in a habitual way, without knowing why or questioning. Stuck on the unending wheel of life's events, they become slaves to their circumstances. They fear their lives will fall apart if they alter their behavior. Resisting change is a powerful mindset, generally unrecognized. It prevents people from an accurate view of their lives and blocks any attempt to deal with it.

Consider the parts of your life that make you unhappy, yet seem impossible to change. It might take an immense sacrifice that would cause upheaval all around you. Perhaps you fear that you couldn't accomplish it... so why try? Instead of tackling the big sacrifice, choose smaller ones. Discover that you can. Then, slowly increase the risk. In the process, you realize you can think and choose a different path. No longer do you default to, "It's too difficult, so why bother?" Buildings are constructed a block at a time; the thousand mile journey begins with a single step.

When you understand this, you can begin to direct your life—reshape yourself, maximize your potential, and impact the world. Or you can stall and let circumstances prevent personal fulfillment.

Will you stagnate or find a way to grow stronger and succeed? Fashion your principles with a discerning mind toward the values of family and culture. Embrace some views and discard others, in order to discover your purpose. Identify and seek experiences that instill confidence to help you learn and grow. Release self-defeating fears. Determine to treat others with compassion and kindness, rather than tearing them down or victimizing them. Each nurturing interaction is a small way of improving the world.

Base your outlook and vision for the future on a realistic assessment of your knowledge, skills, and potential to improve them. This approach goes deeper than positive thinking because your thoughts will lead to plans and action. Examine the adversity you face. Talk about how it makes you feel, what caused it, what consequences may come. Is your perception of the difficulty or obstacle accurate? Are the consequences likely? If you were to argue against your beliefs and perceptions, what would you say? What can you do to change this?

A common example is being cut off in traffic. Your anger flares. You feel disrespected, personally affronted. Does that jerk think he can get away with inconsiderate driving? Distance yourself from your emotions and analyze. Maybe the individual is rushing to an accident a loved one was in. Perhaps he has had an emergency and is on the way to the hospital. That would qualify the slight as unintentional and reveal that your first assumptions were incorrect. You likely won't know, but you can choose to respond to situations without thinking everyone is out to offend you, reason it out and move on.

Core values can't lead to the life you want if they remain unknown.

#IntegrityBook #Integrity

EMPATHY

Experiencing pain, whether physical, social, or emotional is part of life. Learning to deal with it in one area enables you to handle it in other, often extremely painful situations. Humans can endure much when internally programmed to keep going, because the body follows the will. On one hand, some young people with good genetics ruin their bodies and minds through intentionally destructive lifestyles. Others, with disadvantaged genetics or physical challenges, excel far beyond those born with more advantages. Enduring pain can build character. When you discover your limitations, and stretch further, you gain confidence in your capabilities.

Each winter when I was a child, I suffered from respiratory and stomach ailments. My frequent illness led to a full battery of tests, including an extremely painful bone marrow test, which left me with a scar on my hip. However, nothing determined the cause for my sickness which continued year after year. My immunity would drop, leading to pneumonia. Or my stomach would turn against me with a flu or severe infection, and solid food would do more damage than good. I'd have an extended hospital stay with lots of drugs, which at times left me uncertain as to what was real and what wasn't.

Though I didn't mind, I remember being afraid. Pain was just something that happened to me. I never thought I could combat it; it was out of my control. One day I found my will to live, to survive... or die trying.

That year when I was hospitalized I was in such bad shape, it appeared I was dying. My mother, with all her nurses' training, was unable to help me, and cried when she thought I was asleep. I realized she felt my pain. I grasped my connection to her and everyone in my life through invisible bonds, and vice versa. She would have given her life for me in a moment. Yet there was a greater purpose in my suffering—to give me empathy and understanding, a natural conclusion I had while trying to make the best of the circumstances. At that moment, it was sickness and pain.

During that time, I started enjoying comic books. My hospital stay was so long I began nightly "missions" from my room, driven by my powerful imagination and the effects of strong medicine. I'd raid the children's hospital visitation room down the hall which had a closet full of comic books with heroes fighting bad guys. I was learning *how* to fight from my dad, but I was learning why to fight through comic books.

One day my mom brought me *The Savage Sword of Conan the Barbarian*, an adult comic. What joy! The adult label back then meant violent themes. I suspect she assumed all comics were for children. I started to request more.

Conan, a fictitious barbarian, lived in a world of swords and sorcery. A young Arnold Schwarzenegger brought this larger-than-life character to the movie screen in the 1980's. Big and strong, he dealt thoroughly with bad people, often in very final ways. He seemed realistic, not like an idealized super hero who was so good he never did wrong. Raw, vibrant, and ready for adventure, he made some mistakes and at times things didn't go as planned. He plunged into adventure and challenges, and knew how to enjoy himself, despite enduring suffering and slavery.

Fearless and healthy, he was the exact opposite of me. As I imagined being him; he became my fictional role model, a much more fulfilling role than lying in a bed waiting to die. I remained in the hospital for so long one year that my hair grew out and I strongly resisted cutting it. It made me look more like Conan. I kept it long into my teens.

Arnold Schwarzenegger popularized body building, a new sport and developed huge muscles before steroids became common. At that time there were bodybuilders with excellent genetics and others with great grit. My dad was one of those early bodybuilders. Even now he remains connected to key people from the early world of bodybuilding. He was one of the few personal friends of Arthur Jones, the man who invented the Nautilus exercise machines.

Although my dad didn't get great genetics, he became hugely muscled by twenty-five, far more than I've ever achieved. As a young man he was struck by a car while on a motorcycle. Afterward, the doctor said if it wasn't for his muscle and strength, he'd have been paralyzed or worse.

He had the grit and the mental discipline for transformation. This determination overflowed to others; it seemed he had enough for himself and everyone he knew. If there was danger, my dad ran toward it instead of away from it, especially if someone was being taken advantage of. It's no coincidence I made connections to Conan who reminded me of my father.

One day my dad gave an interview to an online forum of strength enthusiasts. He said in the early days of the sport they got energy for exercising from their anger. He could easily turn it on and channel it into the workout, making for very demanding exercise. As I got older, I related; I was built with the same passion. For that, I idolized my dad, a real life hero. The Conan in the comics never turned to mush over the love he had for a woman and his family, like my dad did. He loved openly and completely, never holding back for the people he cared about.

I realized my mother felt my pain, and my father provided an ideal example of health and fitness. These things gave me the decision, grit, and role model for not getting sick like that again. After that time, it stopped. They never knew why or how.

Humans can endure much when internally programmed to keep going, because the body follows the will.

#IntegrityBook #Integrity

CONVICTION

Honesty alone isn't enough to develop integrity. In other words, being frank about limitations or your desire to avoid responsibility doesn't allow you to sidestep it and maintain your integrity. Because honesty *can* bring persecution, it's misunderstood. For instance, the United States was started by those who were open about their religious beliefs and suffered for it. In an effort to live an authentic life without persecution, they left their countries to come here, and face discomfort, loss, and risk. Being forced to live a lie there was worse that the new unknown here.

Honesty can bridge the development of personal integrity, but it's useless unless you to cross over to broader, better character. You move across that bridge by testing your convictions and living them out.

I had a three week, out-of-school case of the flu in high school. I was gone so long I had to go to the school on the weekends to fit back in, although I'd done most of my assignments at home.

My advanced courses were filled with students who had parents that were respected in the community or who had wealth. They were there because they'd been maneuvered into the classes.

My physics course was a perfect example. While the smooth-talking teacher gave special encouragement to the popular kids, he sat me near the front and made frequent comments to me. Only later did I realize he thought I was a troublemaker, because I had long hair. Since I wasn't, his remarks made no sense. He implied that I was a cheat and didn't belong in the class, yet he had no idea how many of his favored students were dishonest. I saw it, but people knew that even if I thought it was wrong, I wouldn't go out of my way to turn them in. My beliefs weren't a weapon against others, although I wouldn't lie to a direct question.

When I came back, our class was doing a group exercise. I didn't understand it and got assigned to the misfits' team, made up of two girls who dressed punk, trying to imitate Madonna, a popular 1990s singer.

We were to build a small bridge out of Popsicle sticks and glue. That's all I understood and my teammates didn't care. Trying to be helpful, I brought more glue and Popsicle sticks the next day, not knowing we were only supposed to use the materials that we were given.

The teacher said in a measured, scholarly voice, "Mr. Bryan, please come to the head of the class." Everyone knew I was in trouble except me. I'd made no attempt to conceal the additional materials, because I had no idea it was against the rules.

And nobody had told me... even as I walked to the front.

"Mr. Bryan, I want you to please take a seat until the end of this class. You have been caught cheating, and not only are you getting a failure grade for this entire semester, you are being expelled from this class, and I am going to suggest that you are suspended from the school for the rest of the year."

I thought he was joking because he sounded so cheerful. However, the silence in the room and the eyes looking away told me he wasn't. He was making me an example. I asked him how I was cheating. I made the case that had I known it was cheating, wouldn't I have been more sneaky?

He would hear none of it.

I went through the rest of the day as normal, and when I got home, I told my parents.

They talked to the principal. The teacher had actually started formal proceedings to have me suspended. My parents went into battle mode, and started setting up meetings, planning on going legally "nuclear" on this teacher and the school. But first, they wanted me to try and talk to him the next morning. They told me to say "I believe that there's been a misunderstanding. My parents would like to have a meeting and work it out."

Surprisingly, he agreed. In fact, it was the first time he talked with me, and not at me. He acknowledged the misunderstanding, said he'd withdrawn his complaint, and let make up the lesson with an extra assignment. I was just as shocked as I was when he accused me of being a cheat.

Later that day, I found out what transpired from two cheerleaders. They heard what had happened through school-wide gossip. The entire cheerleading squad went to him "gave him hell." They said that there was no way that I could have been a cheat and that he had it completely wrong. It was because of them fighting for my reputation and honor that the teacher reversed his decision. With that, my parents were satisfied that the situation was handled.

Honesty alone isn't enough to develop integrity.

#IntegrityBook #Integrity

AWARENESS

While developing integrity, you begin to see the world differently. Many people will proclaim they behave one way and then do the opposite. This gap will become easier and easier to identify. Values will show clearly under pressure, which is a good learning experience for them and others. You can fail in many ways and survive, but integrity in character failure is difficult to recover. You'll learn to see the connection and disconnection between motivations and actions as you evaluate yourself and others.

In my late thirties I was called in for jury duty. A previous call occurred when I was in and out of the country, residing between Florida and Texas, and I received a pass on my duty. This time, I arrived in a business suit, ready to attend a meeting afterward, if the day ended early. I was prepared to serve in any way I could.

During jury selection, the attorneys asked the prospective jury members various questions. This case involved someone harmed or killed in a vehicle accident and the victim was trying to prove fault and get compensation. They told us little else. However, they asked whether or not we could keep an open mind on fault and blame, if one of the drivers was drinking or on drugs.

I realized that I thought very differently from my peers. I believe people *are* responsible for their actions and there is little ambiguity when it comes to *understanding* the law. Of course, there is interpretation when applying it or serving justice. We all know that sometimes the guilty go free and the innocent get convicted. However, understanding the law is fairly simple even if you don't agree with it.

More than one prospective jury member complained of police mistreatment or brutality. A white woman said her daughter had been stopped by the police, supposedly abused and taken to jail. A young black man had a similar story; he was stopped driving and was supposedly abused and taken to jail. They felt they were treated badly.

Why was this astounding? Because they admitted that the treatment followed committing a crime and being caught *red-handed*. They were stopped for drunk driving and believed the police were physically rough on them. Many members of the jury pool appeared not to want to serve. This whole thing was an inconvenience and they didn't mind telling everyone through their words, tone, and body language.

I was stunned. If asked my opinion, I'd have said that if you commit a crime and get caught, you should accept responsibility and the consequences. If the police beat you, find the lesson in that. People screw up, and I can forgive them, but that has nothing to do with justice.

Unfortunately, taking responsibility for one's actions is becoming unfashionable in America. People feeling entitled to success without the necessary effort, and then blame others for their failure. Sadly, I've observed this attitude among many childhood friends, complaining and expecting something for nothing. I wish they'd invested the time and energy spent spinning elaborate explanations of why they didn't get what they feel they should have received, into doing something constructive.

I sat there feeling like a cultural alien, growing nervous. My environment from birth and choice and the territory that comes with extreme experiences, had centered on high-pressure personal growth. Soon I'd be required to answer truthfully about experiences I'd bottled up, a time quite different from the public, white-collar corporate world I was now perfectly comfortable in.

I'd learned not to discuss these things with colleagues early in my career. Many sheep never see the big bad wolf; he exists as a scary children's story, but isn't a reality. They'd be shocked to think someone would take from you or your loved ones on a whim simply to make you suffer, or had a desperate need, and you were the nearest victim, or simply because they thought they could get away with it.

Most individuals believe people out there are doing their best, but *that* best doesn't mean goodwill, or that they respect you and society's rules. Some never learned those rules or those standards were an unavailable luxury because they lived in an environment on the fringes of society. They were rooted outside of the main streams of culture, although at times, like school they were more fully exposed to conventional practices. People physically scarred in childhood often suffer damage to their outlook that mars their ability to respect others.

A person who protects the sheep is always treated with suspicion, because he behaves much like the wolf. Although people have heard of the "wolf," most haven't seen the predator. Officials like police officers, military men, first responders, firemen, and military specialists are protectors of the sheep. In my environment the protectors were the dominant culture, the role model choice.

I was called on. "Have you or anyone in your extended family, witnessed or been a victim of a violent crime?" I started to recount my experiences; I could have told stories for hours. The court reporter's fingers flew over her keys. Everything was videotaped. I thought differently than my peers. It disturbed me to hear their views and shook my confidence I could be an impartial jury member. I was taking too much time and had the impatient attention of everyone in the judge's chambers.

He cut me off. "What I want to know, sir, is could you do your civic duty and serve on the jury with an open mind? This is a yes or no question."

I couldn't say for sure. I felt confused, pressured to give an answer I wasn't comfortable with. My mind and pulse raced. I decided to be truthful, even if it cost me. It felt dangerous not saying what the judge clearly wanted. Not knowing the jury duty rules, I suspected I was breaking them. "When I walked through the door I was completely willing and capable of doing my civic duty; but after telling everyone here all that stuff about my experiences, I'm not sure anymore." It was the best reply I could give.

I think he had sympathy for me, because he accepted my "I don't know" and explained to the jury that in rare and honest cases, this was the appropriate answer. Ironically, though I was called to serve on the jury, the case settled the day we arrived for the trial. Maybe someone didn't like their chances with the jury, especially with one juror who had deep belief in personal responsibility.

PART V:
BENEFITS FOR YOU AND SOCIETY

Serving others can bring incredible, long-lasting benefits and joy. If you're developing integrity by keeping your promises, this simple social commitment builds trust between you and others. These acts demonstrate commitment, your value of others, and the essence of your integrated life approach: reliable communication. When you follow through, you create expectation in others, then exceed those expectations, and say upon completion, "It's done." This is exceptional behavior.

You do this for yourself. Even though it benefits others, their expectation doesn't drive you. Your self-respect and self-value motivate your high level of performance. You find that you anticipate similar behavior from others, but whether or not they meet your expectations, you're content to lead by example.

Your dependability provides a foundation for your

interaction with others. For instance, you'll drive your reliable, old, less status-lifting car instead of your shiny, but poorly-maintained and unreliable Ferrari, because you want to get to work and appointments on time, without the stress of delay or a breakdown. In that same way, reliance secures trust. If someone has similar values and you have proven your dependability, trust between you comes easier and quickly opens doors to opportunity.

Your integrity attracts like-minded people to you when you want to produce and create. Connect your character with discipline, constructive skills, and organizational ability. Use your developed analytical faculties to refine your plan and then establish success by executing it and achieving your objectives.

Your best product comes from the difficult work invested in your most important project of transformation—yourself. Employers, vendors, and employees value well-balanced character, so orchestrate your symphony of skills for repeatable results and greater productivity. Every improvement helps you and those you associate with.

Your transparent life allows family and associates to observe your values, motivations and abilities. Another bonus is that not only have you learned to understand them, but they can more easily understand you. Part of your growth is being candid regarding your weaknesses and your intention to become stronger. Acknowledging your assets creates fertile ground for good business. Even if you fail, your competency will be clear and you'll be rewarded when you make things right.

Doing business with people who share your values lets you focus on your projects without worry about their thoughts and intentions. They'll have little concern about holding you accountable because your commitment to serving them is clear. Your consideration shows when you prioritize their needs and their time constraints.

Your confidence in your ability to do the job eliminates any need to obsess over the success or failure of others. As a result, you'll find it unnecessary and unappealing to participate in corporate or personal gossip, or expose the weaknesses of others; you'll keep confidences without judgment. Being a responsible partner in the workplace, you'll perform well, but not to shame others, because your excellence allows you to be unconcerned about competition.

Your integrity attracts like-minded people to you when you want to produce and create.

#IntegrityBook #Integrity

LEADERSHIP

To achieve a life of value and integrity demands personal transformation. After you clarify your core principles, express them to others, and live them, leadership naturally results. Your transformation attracts friends, colleagues, and customers who desire to increase their own. When they see qualities in you that they admire, you naturally become someone they want to emulate. You do your job with excellence and live with high ethics and deep compassion. Others watch your plans come to fruition. The pleasure you have in goal achievement unlocks the excitement of others in your vision.

Superficial leadership relies on corporate titles and positions. The badge of authority some display is sometimes their only link to their reluctant followers. In traditional leadership the one with the position at the top may own their heads, but not necessarily win their hearts.

Character driven leadership is earned through integrity. With or without a title, this kind of leader draws people to him and creates strong bonds with them. Mutual respect insures enthusiasm for projects and truthful communication.

A façade of agreement with an outward "yes" but an inward "no" only imitates genuine compliance. Do employees speak the truth or only say what is expected? Shallow commitment saturates the entertainment industry where creativity and power through wealth and status has combined with disastrous results. Scores of pop stars inhabit an artificial world of their advisors making. They often lose touch with reality, fail to discern the truth around them, and then forget who they are. They no longer know themselves, strange victims of success, blinded to the fallout of their choices—lost. When their celebrity bubble pops, the media comments briefly, and then moves their attention to the next inflated star.

Leaders with integrity understand life's true reward is their character; they express it through their consistent conduct and commitment to bettering themselves. Success doesn't mean the never-ending pursuit of recognition or the accumulation of material things. Their legacy for their family, friends, followers and the world is their ideals, and their life which inspired others. When outstanding leaders die, they leave a powerful example behind, continued in the people they lived with, worked with, and served. This is far more important than the possessions they accumulated.

Gratitude opens your perspective. You realize that when others view your challenges, they'd see those as difficulties that they'd be happy to face in comparison to their own. Knowing this about them increases your sensitivity to what you believe you deserve and thankfulness for what you have.

This gratitude can't exist with an attitude that the world owes you. When you lose someone or something precious, you learn that those things you took for granted are really on loan, gifts for a time in life. Leaders who lack gratitude and humility lead poorly. They make decisions at the expense of others, instead of in service to them, putting others at risk just to increase their own profits.

Gratitude upholds principled leaders by creating an atmosphere of clarity and better decisions. Difficulties can be viewed as possibilities rather than confusing and chaotic situations to avoid or escape. A grateful person handles reality and makes the best of it without brooding or getting stuck. I try to practice gratitude every day by reminding myself of what I am thankful for.

Trusting, honest leaders are easy to get to know. They welcome two-way conversations and readily talk to others, seeking mutual understanding. They differ from people who become obsessed with their own image after moving up to higher levels of power. Those people put up barriers in an attempt to protect their position.

Although you are the living representation personal standards or a corporate image, a role model shouldn't constantly market his positions. People like that always talk and rarely listen or ask others questions. Their outgoing box overflows, but their incoming box is closed.

Leaders often separate their professional and private lives. Appropriate distance is healthy to maintain respect, but not so much as to be unfriendly, thus becoming a person others can't get to know or identify with. An authentic approachability surrounds a leader with integrity.

Leadership requires good people skills in order to focus on others without performing or presenting. A mind trained to ask good questions paired with skilled listening fine tunes your intuition as you pay attention to the other person. During the process you sift the information others give including what they say, how they say it, and what they eventually do. You discern by sight, sound, and body language a more complete message than simply the spoken word.

As you compare and analyze the information you can offer positive reinforcement and use each situation as an opportunity to help others reach their potential. The result is clear communication freed of constraints that some people employ to avoid accountability. Your manner and style in interactions will help eliminate in others attempts at using deceptive language.

PROTECTION

Integrity doesn't eliminate occasions of false blame. Transparency simplifies life and you don't waste time doubting yourself. Even when your integrity is questioned, you understand how to be assertive and accept the consequences even if you are blamed for the actions of another.

Sometimes, because life isn't fair, you suffer the extreme discomfort and distress of an attack on your integrity. In those situations you choose to continue to follow the rules. If the truth were to be printed in the newspaper for all to see, the result might be very different. Even during the course of such events you can hold onto the principle that doing your best is something you own, that cannot be taken from you.

In my first job out of college, I had no marketable skills. I was hired because I walked door-to-door job hunting using a list I'd made from the local yellow pages. One business had a part-time young man answering phones and doing odd tasks. They weren't pleased with him because he'd given them a short notice to go on a church-related trip abroad. As soon as I walked in the door, they fired him.

They made computer software for the agricultural industry, a small business going through all the lessons that small businesses do. They had me answer phones, straighten the office, do really anything for a decent wage. I had no software skills, but I could operate a computer and I learned fast.

The agricultural industry is tough; the company was always trying to make ends meet. They said they were a family company, in fact they told me the first day they preferred to hire people with children or family, "because they stick around." They didn't want to invest in employees who'd be more likely to abandon them for a better job or wage. I understood that.

They could choose their plans and policies and anyone who didn't like it could leave. They valued honesty and openness. If you had a skill or interest that could help the business, and were dependable, they were willing to let you try it to benefit yourself and the business. I appreciated the opportunity and freedom to grow, because if I performed well, I'd progress and get more experience.

With no previous training, I learned to create software from the bottom up. I worked my way through the ranks, teaching myself the basics of software creation at night and on weekends, without formal training or outside classes. However, I did take a semester at a local community college, which was strange because I had a four-year degree.

I wanted a career change when I realized my first degree wasn't marketable. At the two-year school, I enrolled in all the computer-related courses, including one on the basics of programming. Because I was learning faster on the job, my first semester was my last one. I barely finished it because I was so busy teaching myself.

Through the connections of one of the owners, I got a complete discounted set of books on the programming language we used at work, and accelerated my knowledge. The texts were outrageously expensive, hundreds of dollars, difficult for me to afford. Soon after though, I went from testing software to coding and fixing software, making me a billable employee. Now my time investment at work could be billed to a client. I began producing a direct profit for the company when I worked on an account.

The job was high-pressure, high stakes and stressful. The owners made it very clear to me that billable time was best for the company, and for my future position in it. They only wanted me to do pay time activities—the most valuable use of my time for them.

Employees on the pay-time fast track were strictly monitored and required to account for every fifteen minutes of their time. They mandated a good and realistic description for every quarter hour except lunch which ingrained a highly developed sense of time and the use of it. The pressure was unrelenting; it kept us moving, planning ahead, and insuring there was always a valuable task to do.

However, the company's culture of honesty and openness had an interesting twist. The partners verbalized how they felt about you in any given moment, especially if it was negative, for this tended to be a high-pressure environment. They "let off steam" as a result of inevitable disagreements and friction. They balanced dishing out hostile insults with the general understanding that you could give it right back. However, rarely did anyone first say something insulting and hostile to a partner.

Once I was called into a partner's office. He reviewed my timesheets he subjected me to a barrage of questions about why I'd spent so much time on no-pay and unbillable activities. Surprised by his insults, I reminded him that *he* had specifically requested me to do those tasks. It wasn't what he wanted to hear, but I refused to be abused.

As we traded remarks in an "honest and open" manner, heated responses propelled us to our feet. We were primed to tear his office apart (he was a big guy and former football player.) I was ready to fight, no matter the outcome; it was obvious I wouldn't take his abuse.

I was always grateful for these lessons. Early in my

career I learned to not let things bother me, to separate personal from business and never confuse the two. A small company may say, "We're family oriented. We'll take care of you." As a result they may even ask you to forego your bonus for the good of the family company, but if the company/family suffers they'll let you go. It's just business, nothing personal.

In this environment of borderline abuse, I quickly grasped that employment was a partnership. My continuing employment wasn't simply to please the boss. I was there to learn, do a good job, gain experience and be recognized for it. This was an important shift in understanding.

Four years later, while working with Europeans, I learned that Americans typically work for the sake of working, but Europeans work to enhance their lives and the lives of their families. Advertisers in America work hard to persuade us that material possessions make life good. We forget about the quality of life, the quality of time, and our own needed enrichment. Then one day our employer drops us like a sack of rocks, and we lose our identity.

In my partnership, I decided to ensure my own life enrichment and create balance. While working like a maniac helped my employer, it also gave me valuable experience and skills. I recorded all my accomplishments and constantly reworked my resume to keep it market ready. I wanted to make sure I was always building upon something.

Eventually they assigned me to an extremely important job where reliability was critical. I was to go to client locations and deploy new code, but more importantly, do database upgrades. This was like brain surgery in magnitude, with the procedure already mapped out. All I had to do was follow instructions explicitly and not make any mistakes. This high-pressure task was done during commercial season, because the agricultural processing plants would shut down entirely while I did it. Normally they ran non-stop twenty-four hours a day. The planned downtime for my visits would cost thousands of dollars, more if there were complications.

One time when I went to deploy new code, the day started like a routine day. I arrived at the largest client location before the sun rose. I passed through security and went through clearance and into the computer room to start. It was always colder in there so that the computers would run efficiently without overheating. They had some very old equipment the size of a washing machine (and looking like one) purchased decades earlier for huge sums of money. This client had computerized from the beginning.

I prepared while I watched the clock for the scheduled maintenance time. I went through all the software processes, noting the code on the monitor flash by as the deployment program rapidly changed the "brain" of the entire processing plant. During this time-consuming process all you do is observe and wait for errors after each step, and nervously hope everything goes well, so you can begin the next step.

It went well, each operation flowing just like I'd practiced. Although it was routine, it was never so routine that I got lazy. I had checklists for my checklists, and backup plans for my backup plans. Being thoroughly prepared was necessary. I was only going through the tasks looking for something unusual to happen, and it did. The last step didn't work, and it gave me errors that indicated the package I was provided to deploy was having problems.

However, I had an identical copy, which was expected for this job. I used this copy just in case there was a problem with the storage. Perhaps a scratch on the CD I was using caused an issue; sometimes media and storage fails. I repeated the process, having alerted my superiors it would take a little longer, as I was working through an unforeseen problem.

The problem resurfaced, even with the backup, which was an extremely bad thing. It meant that whatever was prepared for me was the problem, existing inside the identical copies I was provided... or something extremely unusual was happening – as rare as a lightning bolt strike. Once again, I alerted my superiors and started troubleshooting.

I had a copy of the raw package before it was prepared for me, my extra backup plan, my decision, not a requirement. I went through the motions of preparing the code as my immediate boss would have done; it was his responsibility to prepare the code for deployment. When I prepared the code, it went well, but when I tried to apply it, the system told me it was bad code. It was like baking a cake. You have all the ingredients, have prepared them many times, but when you make the cake it falls apart. It implodes when you bake it. This made no sense.

The whole situation became an emergency. People were literally screaming, calling my bosses, and nothing worked. I tried everything. My immediate boss said he was on his way to help. He was trying to keep calm, and I was calm, but incredibly stressed. I'd never had a situation like this. I felt like I was missing something very basic and told him this.

He said, "Don't do anything. Just wait for me."

He implied that my troubleshooting might make matters worse. My stress increased, but the problem was beyond my skill with the tools I had.

He arrived and said, "Go home." He assumed responsibility and pointedly dismissed any assistance I might offer.

I left. Soon after I learned he had everything up and running, that there was no longer a problem.

The next day I was demoted; deployments at client locations were no longer my responsibility. The owners were figuring out what my next role should be. Nobody explained what the problem was, or if I'd done something wrong. No one would even talk to me about it. Clearly, I was being blamed.

I thought long and hard about what happened, and why.

The previous week my immediate boss discussed trying something new during deployments to make the process more efficient. It wasn't the process that was in the technical guidance of the programming language, but he believed it would work because the preparation processes worked normally.

If this was like baking a cake, *this* was an ingredient substitution. Unfortunately since everything appeared to bake correctly, he couldn't know if it was successful unless he tasted it (tried it out at a client location). He used me to test an idea, and then let me take the blame when it failed.

My boss had risen quickly in the company and become a trusted partner. He worked hard, long hours. People, including himself, claimed he put in eighteen to twenty hour days. I'd come in as early as 4:00 a.m. for an early start on work, or my studying and testing, because I had a lot to learn and achieve. He'd arrive around 4:10 am, and not knowing I was there, would "work" for about three hours playing video games. I caught him and witnessed him failing to correct people who commended him for his long hours.

Months passed and no one explained what happened. I couldn't state my suspicions about my superior without complications, but I saved the backups. If I ever got the chance to use them, I planned to prove they were improperly prepared. Unfortunately, proving a mistake with a code package is harder than proving an ingredient substitution in a cake.

I was never asked my side of what happened. Years later I heard from multiple people that he'd betrayed the company owners. True or not, I don't remember the details; I just know many people told the story. That kind of talk hurts your reputation and can kill your career. Did he let the blame fall on me? I don't know. I do know he was a man without integrity.

Transparency simplifies life and you don't waste time doubting yourself.

#IntegrityBook #Integrity

COMPASSION

Compassion blooms with integrity, because it grows out of experiencing hardship, pain and sorrow. With self-reflection on these, you become aware of the strong human connection we all have, and acquire the capacity for empathy, benevolence and kindness. You externalize the value of your integrity and wisdom to others. You see their worth or potential and feel compelled to help them along their path. You find ways to provide them opportunities to succeed through professional service to your clients, and through common tenderness to your fellow man. This rare gift provides as much pleasure to the giver as the receiver.

Sometimes people ask for your opinion. A compassionate response frames the answer in the form of a critique. This includes positive and negative parts with the emphasis on the positive. It targets what could be done, what could be improved upon, as well as what was done wrong. This kind of response differs from simply pointing out errors, although identifying the undesirable can equip someone to correct and avoid the same mistake. However, a one-sided discouraging response fails to inspire others to improve by expressing confidence in their ability and motivation to improve.

Wanting to treat others as you wish to be treated means investing the extra effort to deliver helpful instruction, not just dish out criticism. Negativity saps strength and drains energy. Positivity renews, nurtures and encourages others. Look for the good in people and then state it clearly to them and as appropriate, to others. Find things to praise in those around you and celebrate their achievements.

In the tale of the owner training his donkey, the rider dangles a carrot on the end of a stick in front of his beast. The goal is get the donkey to move ahead with a positive incentive. The owner also has a stick if the carrot doesn't work, a negative incentive as a different way to prompt the donkey in the right direction. Most people use the stick which is easier. Using the carrot requires time and creativity.

The carrot, or positive reward, benefits the receiver and the giver. For this reason, it's impossible to invest effort and service to affirm the virtuous in another without having the same qualities. Those who bring benefits into the world multiply their effects and abilities to inspire, encourage, and heal. Noble feelings come by default when helping others. These efforts are far more effective for lasting change, and once they become habitual, and it grows easier to look for the good and not the bad.

In my third grade class there was a girl, who like me, didn't have to pay tuition. In some ways she was "wild," with little control over her actions. When she was happy, she was ecstatic, but when she was unhappy, she acted out. When someone paid attention to her, she was fun and likable.

One day she was there in the morning, but gone the rest of the day. The same thing happened the next day. Then she was out the rest of the week. I started to watch more closely. She'd arrive, talk to the Bad Teacher, get a handful of books, and go. Instead of leaving by the classroom door, she went through a side door into a neighboring classroom.

During play time one morning, the teacher left the room. I went into the neighboring classroom to find out where the girl had gone. It was quiet. However, the glow of a small lamp kept it from being pitch-black. I navigated the old tables, student desks, cabinets and miscellaneous stacked items. The light came from one of the large boxes.

A refrigerator box was configured around a single student desk and chair, with a door cut in it, and a lamp attached to the top. The girl sat absentmindedly doing homework. I said hello and talked to her. This was obviously some sort of punishment. I don't know what she did, but she didn't get upset or question it, as if she was used to being sent away.

After that I tried to go talk to her in the next room when I could. When she told the teacher I was coming to see her, she was no longer sent to the dark room for the whole day anymore. I don't know if the box was used again, but every time I saw her after that, she wasn't "wild" around me. She even said she thought I was nice.

Those who bring benefits into the world multiply their effects and abilities to inspire, encourage, and heal.

#IntegrityBook #Integrity

ACTION

Sometimes integrity means you must go to battle. It may be required in your professional life or simply because you're compelled to take a stand for others. This isn't to rob them of the valuable lessons hardships bring, but to intervene when they are overpowered and or are victims and need someone stronger to help. Taking a stand has consequences for you and the person you attempt to help.

You might bear their punishment, becoming a sacrificed martyr. Your efforts might seem to change nothing. You might even get killed. However, your willingness to put yourself in harm's way for another, will probably startle the abuser. It will give you something that didn't exist before you stepped up—a little influence and control over the situation you witnessed. Your actions will shout your character and compassion.

In eleventh grade we had three lunch periods. I sat with the outcasts, the nerds. I had long hair which was unfashionable unless you listened to heavy metal. I also liked classical music, so I was *really* weird.

I got interested in it when I was little and my grandparents gave my brother and me a bunch of old stuff they didn't want. Lucky for us, there were old World War II military uniforms, medals and keepsakes... and a record collection of classical music, military anthems, and marches. We dressed up and had battles all over the house. When I was "shot" while the classical music was playing, I'd drop in a dramatic death pose and take a nap—for realism.

Repeated sessions of that extended play made us associate classical music and military marches with war. Some of the albums had pictures of Napoleon-era battle scenes. Their dramatic images showed soldiers fighting and dying with smoke on the battlefield, and horses with wild eyes. Classical music, one more thing that set me apart, has stuck with me ever since.

Our lunchroom served as an events space with a podium and stage on one end. The cafeteria was on the other end with all the student tables arranged on either side of the room with a walkway down the middle. The high-school subcultures and cliques grouped together, laying stake to their favorite spots. Football players and cheerleaders ate opposite my group of friends. However, the place to return our trays and exit was beside them. In order to leave, we had to walk past them, scrutinized like unwilling participants in a fashion show.

A severely handicapped student in our class usually ate near the exit. The football players developed a habit of teasing him, joking and throwing food at him.

One day, they invited him to sit at their table and made jokes to his face accompanied by hysterical laughter. It was horrible. The lunchroom supervisors chose to be oblivious. I thought he might be happy simply for the attention. I suspected that he had no idea that he was being made into a clown at his own expense and didn't realize he was the object of their cruel jokes. It was very wrong.

People at nearby tables remarked loudly, wondering why no one intervened. Someone yelled to a teacher to stop it. The teacher kept his back to the scene and ignored it, engrossed in conversation with another teacher. Student horror increased with the escalating spectacle.

The football players continued making fun of him. The cheerleaders laughed uncomfortably, trapped by social mores of high school acceptance. I started getting mad. Then one of the football players threw food on him.

The handicapped student kept asking "Are you my friend?" trying to shake their hands.

Nearby a student said loudly, "Someone should stop them."

At this point, a football player wrapped his hand in

a napkin making a show of his disgust, and then shook the handicapped student's hand, mocking him by repeating his question every time he asked, "Are you my friend?"

I stood. The metal feet of my chair scraped against the waxed floor, loud in the sudden silence. I headed toward them. It was obvious I wasn't returning my tray—it remained on the table. I crossed the "no-man's land" between the two halves of the lunchroom with every eye on me.

When the football players saw me coming, they tensed. Though I was headed straight towards them, I focused on the student, seeing red. My anger raged inside, but awareness of the crowd made me control of my temper and forced me to come up with a plan. I'd never liked attention, and now I had the spotlight. This could go very badly.

I walked up behind him, put my hand on his shoulder and said a forceful "Hey!" I pretended no one else was there; I ignored them when they asked what I was doing. I wouldn't even give them the satisfaction of looking at them.

I said, "Don't you realize these people are *not* your friends? Don't you realize they are *not* being nice to you, that they are humiliating you for their own amusement?"

I practically yelled, making sure everyone heard me. If you're going to risk, risk big. My anger increased my volume. Stunned silence continued.

Then teachers rushed over; worried a fight might

break out. The handicapped kid appeared confused, trying to figure out what was going on. He only knew that the laughter had ended. He really had no idea what they'd done, which made me feel better, but someone should have protected him and since no one moved—by God, I did.

I stared at the football players, shook my head in disbelief, and left them in shock. I wanted to do this before the teachers attempted to restore order, which ironically, would have probably have started a fight. Sometimes people act very tough when they're held back.

As I walked away I knew I was screwed. They'd retaliate because I humiliated one of the school "kings."

Someone said, "Oh sh*t."

I got my tray and turned it in. I was a dead man walking in this high school. People shied away. They didn't talk to me. It was like I was radioactive.

I waited outside for the bell to ring to return to class. Alone.

In moments, the entire football team came after me. Their leader, whom I later learned was the quarterback, had a name similar to mine, "Kolby." They approached me as a group. I stood and walked towards them. There was no way I'd let them trap me against a wall, in a subservient position. It went against all my instincts to sit, cornered. I obeyed my intuition.

I squared off against the quarterback, who could

have crushed me, waiting for him to make the first move. I'd stopped exercising a few years earlier and with puberty got taller, but stayed the same weight. I was a skinny, long-haired kid trying to deal with my genetics; I couldn't gain weight no matter how much I ate.

He said that they weren't making fun of the handicapped student and meant no harm, seeking my approval. I felt immediate relief. This was better than getting squashed like a bug. He was a good leader, and I didn't remember him making fun of the handicapped student, but he didn't try to stop it. Now he felt responsible for his team's actions and his conscience was kicking in. His little speech was an attempt to put a harmless spin on what had happened. He wanted to save himself and his team embarrassment as football players and the popular guys in our class.

His teammates had other plans. One punched me in the arm as I spoke to him. Another shoved me towards Kolby, and yelled "Kick his ass, Kolby!" When I tried to walk away, they stopped me.

Kolby kept trying to reason his way out of this humiliation.

This fueled new anger. I interrupted him. "This is bullsh*t! You can't stand there and tell me to my face that you weren't making the joke at his expense. You were making fun of him to his face, and *everyone* saw it. What you are telling me is *bull sh*t*."

I walked away, certain I would get punched in

the back of my head, but nothing happened, and I never had trouble after that. I discovered I'd earned the respect of all the cheerleaders, and one even had a crush on me—an unexpected turn of events for an awkward teenager.

Your actions will shout your character and compassion.

#IntegrityBook #Integrity

PART VI:
STRIVING FOR INTEGRITY

Although the school system teaches knowledge, it doesn't teach life skills. Without discounting the need for information, what counts is learning to conduct ourselves in society. Unfortunately, these critical life skills fall at the feet of increasingly busy parents who often both work and are tired or distracted. On the other hand, it's never too late to learn these lessons, and the events of the past can prepare people to gain the wisdom from them.

This book reveals nothing new about building character, integrity, or being a good person. These truths have permeated many cultures for centuries with differing emphases. Despite differences in culture and religion, the longevity of these principles reinforce the ethics that personal development of character and integrity transcends time and culture.

Whether people live before or after technological advancement, they remain the same inside. We can choose high standards whether young or old, in vastly different settings.

Character improvement has no shortcuts; it takes concentration and time. This book suggests no quick methods, but rather encourages readers to pursue a lifelong process. It is about the journey, realizing that day-to-day challenges contain grains and nuggets of the ultimate prize—the satisfaction of who you become and how you impact others.

There's no magic formula, no twelve-step program. You earn integrity. In the process you discover other good qualities that are part of the total package: honesty, respect, goodness, commitment, hard work, reliability and, of course, keeping your word. In fact, striving isn't just the hard work; it's the source of gratification throughout life that you can become a worthy person. Ultimately, you do it for yourself. It's nice to be acknowledged, but nothing compares to the peace of mind kind you gain from facing pain, disappointment, even rejection and overcoming rather than succumbing. An integrated person must go through hard things to fulfill his potential.

I love the saying, "You make life happen or it happens to you." Integrity isn't simply measured by outward signs of achievement. A person may not have masses of goods, but be a person who does much good, and who is full of goodness. Integrity isn't a reward like a medal that you put on display. It describes your approach to life, your strategy, your choices—not your techniques.

I believe that if I don't continue to push myself, I'll lose control and something will happen I don't want.

If you're not intentionally challenging yourself to become better, neglect can erode your integrity. Remain aware; sharpen your perception of yourself, your surroundings and your world. Improve your strengths as well as your weaknesses. Seek the positive in adversity; learn what you're made of. Be honest, but also be encouraged by what you discover.

Friends who compete in gaming or sport, share the same pattern of fearful withdrawal from life when they think they'll compete less often. In their minds the stakes get higher when they aren't competing as often and they risk less and less. It's a common response. Challenges sharpen us. We need seasons and people to relax with, but we grow through goals, appropriate risks and friendly competition. Sitting back too long isn't necessarily comfort.

Relief and happiness differ. Release from pain doesn't guarantee happiness, nor does the excitement and adrenaline rush of challenge mean you're happy. But it may mean you're comfortable.

Life is like a river, and you're in it. You move forward faster or slower depending how close you are the sluggish waters of the bank or if you're in the rushing flow of the center stream. You will go somewhere, not stopping as long as you're still alive.

Like the river, time continues to flow. You're born and you'll die like all of humanity. You can grow, the natural and appropriate response to life, or stagnate or get stuck when you hit a rock. You can learn swimming skills and paddle faster or learn to dive and enjoy the depths of the river.

There will be pain. You choose. Will you suffer more for regrets or just keep the scars of overcoming the obstacles you conquered? Much of this is up to you.

You can succeed in spite of yourself through your behavior. Consider two people going down the river and both believe they can't avoid the rocks. They expect to get hurt, that collisions are inevitable, and that it will always happen to them.

One is so overwhelmed by this *fact of life* that he becomes paralyzed. He floats down the river, strike rocks, gets wounded and flounders. He goes under water, tossed back and forth, spinning without bearings. One blow stuns him and instead of preparing to avoid the next, he concentrates on the pain, only to be pounded again. The battering drains his hope, and strips him of any belief that things could change. He never escapes, rests, or gets away from the life pattern of *striking rocks*. He slowly dies.

The other is overwhelmed by this *fact of life* but he wonders if he could somehow avoid the rocks, or do something to reduce the damage they inflict. He begins to prepare for the next hard encounter and come up with ways to miss the rock or minimize his wounds. He realizes some body parts could absorb the blows better than others, offering a way to manage the inevitable blows. He begins to analyze what happens each time he hits a rock, how he struck it, where he got hurt and how quickly he escaped battering. He makes a plan to deal with the next hard encounter. He learns that recovery can provide skills to see ahead and evade the next obstacle. What was once random and unseen can be discovered and avoided.

He gains skill in handling pain, realizes it's temporary, then focuses on the in between time without pain to strategize. Pretty soon his skill reduces the number of impacts and the need to recover. Looking ahead becomes second nature. Steering clear of rocks becomes a skill. Pain becomes less of a concern and the rocky water less of a daily threat.

Having a plan for the rocks in your river enables you to minimize the wounds in life.

With a basic survival plan, you'll negotiate the river of life better. Others will be more willing to assist you on your journey, unafraid that you'll pull them into your drowning embrace. Those people who constantly drift have little more initiative than dead fish. As the saying goes, "Any dead fish can float downstream. Only the live ones can swim against the current." Keep swimming.

PART VII:
STRIVING FOR MEANING

You can only have integrity when your life has meaning. Developing it is a constant commitment to choice, just like embracing life as a whole is a choice. When I was fifteen, I wanted to know the meaning of life. I had many questions and few answers so out of my frustration to find out, I read books on world religions, determined to get an answer. I opened a dozen books around me in a half circle and started reading them all page by page, trying to find something, anything to reveal the meaning for my existence. I read until I had a headache and fell asleep.

I woke up to an insight I hadn't expected. It wasn't a one line explanation which would have been narrow and restricted. I realized I had to live to discover it. Life *is* an experience, a stage where you write and perform your own play. It holds the meaning you bring to it.

I expected a book to give me the answer, when by being born and existing—I had to provide the answer. Every day, every minute, life delivers opportunities by means of challenges and choices. Whether we take the responsibility to engage and choose or whether we happily answer these questions through our effort, the questions are always asked, and the opportunities continue until we die. Our greatest choice is to embrace life, fully living every day that we have.

We all have a footprint, and leave invisible tracks in our wake—our interactions with others, all of the people on our journey. Everyone participates and co-creates his destiny. Sometimes your choice is to accept what is, other times the best decision is transformation or change.

Everyone's drama is unique, for even the view that life is terrible and worthless has some meaning if you stop to recognize it. Living means there is always hope, even in the worst of circumstances. Developing integrity grants you the toughness to proclaim that every difficult occasion can be a stepping stone to a better future.

Nobody can take this from you: your life has meaning. You can develop integrity as the core of many strong character traits. Every day holds multiple opportunities to reinforce your vision for your life and establish admirable ethics and values. Your experiences are yours alone, for your have uniquely experienced them. Joy and sorrow, pride and regrets, achievement and failure blend together on the stage of your life. Whether your audience is large or small, play your part well.

When you view life in terms of questions that you discover answers to, you find new comprehension of pleasure and pain—for you understand that meaning is discovered in all of it. The way you live will answer your most penetrating questions.

Start where you are today and evaluate what you can do to develop your core principles. Take the time to define your personal, unique meaning. Write out your questions and begin the search for your answers. Always approach each day fully engaged with what it brings. Choose a life of meaning, to develop a principled life. Develop a life of integrity.

Every day, every minute, life delivers opportunities by means of challenges and choices.

#IntegrityBook #Integrity

ABOUT KOBY BRYAN

Koby is a Florida native and software consultant, a drummer, an artist, a voracious reader, and a dog lover. His ancestors were action-tested military men that came to Florida to help start a pre-Disney attraction called Cypress Gardens. They were the proud sons and daughters of both the tough Irish on one side; and Arkansas bootleggers on the other. His uncle was a magician, his neighbor owned a Bengal Tiger, he was indirectly struck by lightning, and had a dog that could climb trees so he built it a treehouse. He has had an unusual life, and plans to keep on living it to its fullest.

He was raised with a simple truth: Action speaks louder than words. He became a man by making it his personal mission to deeply understand, inspire and encourage the best from the people in his life.

PLEASE VISIT

about.me/kobybryan